A Jump Ahead

Jen Marsden Hamilton

From Basics to
BIG JUMPS

Be a Star!

Jen

Saddletops Publications

First Published in 2017
by
Saddletops Pty Ltd
T/A Horses and People Magazine
PO Box 99
ROSEWOOD, QLD 4340
AUSTRALIA

www.horsesandpeople.com.au

Editing and Design by
Horses and People Magazine and Liz Hardy Design
Illustrations (unless specified) by Cristina Wilkins

Printed by IngramSpark

ISBN: 978-0-6481195-0-0

Cover Photos: Jen Marsden riding Wee Geordie. Branchville New Jersey. Puissance 6'6". Photo credit: Budd. Walking the course photo credit: Angie Ivory. Top right photo credit: Ana Rattery. Middle right photo credit: Olivia Waddy. Bottom right: Monica Oakley. Photo credit: Take the Moment Photography.

Edited and Published by Horses and People Magazine, Australia. Co-designed with Liz Hardy Design, Canada. Photo credit: Liz Hardy. The content and illustrations first appeared in a series of articles in Horses and People Magazine and have been adapted for publication in this format.

To order copies of *A Jump Ahead* visit: www.horsesandpeople.com.au/shop/products

This book is dedicated to
James Brian Hamilton

I have a fortunate life. I grew up in Schenectady, New York in the 1960's. The 60's were a very exciting time. For a horse crazy girl, it was the beginning of the equestrian world opening up. In 1956 women were finally allowed to jump at the Olympics!

My parents, Loys and James Marsden, encouraged excellence and gave me the best ever Christmas present in 1963 — lessons with George H. Morris. They also had the vision to send me to The Albany Academy for Girls in Albany, New York.

Miss Harris, Headmistress at the Academy, was an exceptional woman and her approach to learning and life was way ahead of the times. One day I was called into her office and given factual, straightforward, and loving advice. I can't remember her exact words but I'll never forget their meaning:

Jen, you have a passion for horses and a talent for riding and jumping horses high. This is exciting for you. But I think there is more in it for you. Your passion, talent, and hard work will only take you so far.

Passion and talent are useless without combining exceedingly correct hard work, compassion, education, and direction. If you personally put all these things together, who knows where your life will lead you!

I do remember two of Miss Harris' sentences from that day and they are etched in my memory:

Jen, if something is easy you're not striving hard or high enough. Raise the pole!

I believed Miss Harris then and I still do. I've used her thoughtful words and they have directed me on an interesting and happy journey and life.

I was fortunate to have supportive parents, nice horses, excellent equestrian teaching, and an education/university degrees BUT Miss Harris didn't mention the most important element:

A partner to encourage, support mentally, emotionally, and financially, and believe in me.

Brian is a teacher and takes great joy in learning, personally doing, and showing others how "to do." He has a quiet vision which he seamlessly

passes on to others. Brian passed his passion for teaching to me.

I love watching horses and riders improve and enjoy "their doing." Brian has always encouraged and supported me in my passion for horses and the sharing of it through teaching.

This book is dedicated to my husband of almost 50 years and hopefully many more.

Brian, you have enhanced my life in so many ways. Thank you.

Jill Swain and Jen Marsden Hamilton. Photo credit: Carolyn Hazel.

Table of Contents

Jen Marsden Hamilton and George H. Morris. Niagra Falls. Canada. Photo credit: Megan Lorius.

The American equestrian George H. Morris is a world icon.

As a junior rider, he won both the American Horse Show Association and the Alfred B. Maclay Equitation Finals. He has also represented the United States internationally and was a member of the USET silver medal team at the Rome Olympics in 1960.

Over the last 5 decades, George's passion for the sport has been directed towards teaching, being the chef d'equipe of the USET (winning team and individual medals at the Olympics and World Equestrian Games), and writing. His first book Hunter Seat Equitation *(1971), set the standard for future equestrian books. In 2015 he published* Unrelenting. *In 2016, George was the coach of the Brazilian show Jumping Team in Rio de Janerio.*

George H. Morris conducts clinics all over the world. He is known for his toughness in maintaining the correct riding basics and classical approach to all disciplines of the equestrian sport.

Foreword

By George H. Morris

Au Sable Forks, New York, now Lake Placid. Ronnie Mutch, whom I'd grown up with at the Ox Ridge Hunt Club, called and asked if I could teach a girl in Schenectady, New York on my way back and forth to my home in New Cannan, Connecticut. Her name was Jen Marsden and her parents, Loys and Jim.

Our first lesson was before Christmas, 1963. It was my first official payment as a professional horseman. I believe my fee was $7.50 per lesson. Jen has a copy of the canceled cheque. My... How times have changed!

While Jen was short of stature, she had all the goods: a great worker, aggressive, brave, soft yet very strong, smart, and dead-eye accurate to the fence. At the time, her two main horses were Wee Geordie and Winter Fair, the first being an open jumper and the latter a hunter/equitation horse. Jen was certainly one of the best riders across the board at that time - hunter, jumper, equitation.

Jen's chestnut mare, to be frank, was a great equitation horse but an average hunter. Bert de Némethy had taught us "striding" with the jumpers. I had an epiphany at the Ox Ridge Junior Spring Show (1964). I tried striding with Jen and her mare that weekend and she won every class. I truly believe Jen Marsden was the first to apply striding in the hunter/equitation divisions.

Jen, of course, was a most successful competitor in all those divisions on the East Coast, up to and including Madison Square Garden. Her riding career morphed into a great teaching career.

Jen Marsden Hamilton is a teaching icon across Canada and New Zealand. She has always had a passion, both for the sport and the horses. I am so pleased and proud that Jen is carrying on my passion for the horse and teaching riders responsibility and correctness. Both the horse and the rider will benefit greatly.

George H. Morris

Clarke Johnstone riding Orient Express were members of the Bronze medal winning New Zealand team at the 2010 World Equestrian Games in Kentucky, USA. Photo credit: Barbara Thomson Photography.

Clarke Johnstone is a three day eventing rider from New Zealand. Originally from the South Island, Clarke is now based near Cambridge in the North Island after returning home from several years based in Europe.

He represented New Zealand at the 2010 World Equestrian Games in Kentucky where they won team bronze and at the 2016 Rio Olympics where Clarke placed individually 6th, riding the beautiful Balmoral Sensation. Other highlights of his career include winning the New Zealand Advanced Eventing Championships three times and being the youngest ever winner of an Eventing World Cup Qualifier at 19 years of age. He also won the 2011 FEI World Cup Eventing Series. Clarke show jumps to Grand Prix level and is a member of the NZ show jumping squad.

Foreword

By Clarke Johnstone

I remember Jen Hamilton teaching me, as a junior rider, the reason that we must pay attention to the small details in our training is so that, when we are competing and the pressure comes on, the small details take care of themselves. "Practice them until they become automatic," she says. "The correctness of your position, the accuracy of your lines, the shape of the corners…." Looking back on my experience at the Rio 2016 Olympics, it makes sense to me more than ever. In our sport, winning or losing almost always comes down to the small details. Whether you had the horse straight before the vertical or if you came to the oxer on the inside line rather than the outside one.

I was very fortunate that I met Jen Hamilton early in my riding career. I was nearly 13 when I started (which Mum was pleased about because by then, I was old enough to catch the pony and tack up by myself), and I was immediately drawn to jumping. Show jumps, cross country jumps, gates or anything else I could find. I was a sponge for information on the subject, so of course, when the renowned Canadian show jumping trainer Jen Hamilton came to give a clinic in Dunedin, in the South Island of New Zealand, I couldn't wait to attend. How exotic!

At the time I was, like most young boy riders, interested in jumping, going fast and having fun, rather than schooling the horses or ponies. Around the same time as I began training with Jen, I had been horrified by a visiting dressage trainer who had suggested that I should be schooling in the arena four days a week! Jen's style of training was very structured, and although I very quickly came to realise the importance (probably above all else), of having a great structure in your training, it was quite different to what I was used to at the time.

During Jen's lessons, she almost always asks her students one particular question before they begin to work over the poles, "When was the last time you practiced stride control?" Of course, during my first lesson I answered incorrectly, I'm not sure I even knew what stride control was, but after a couple of Jen's eagerly awaited visits to Dunedin, I was always able to answer correctly. "The last time I practised stride control was the last time I rode!" As time has gone on and my riding career has progressed, I often think back to that simple question and how absolutely right Jen is.

Jen began staying in our home when she gave her Dunedin clinics and it was then that my family and I found that, as well as a brilliant show jumping trainer, Jen is a warm and generous person and a gifted story teller. The experiences that Jen has had travelling the world with horses and coaching range from amazing to absolutely hilarious.

One of my favourite stories was her retelling of the time one very brave person described Jen as "rugged and sturdy." Jen can be quite fearsome at times, and I bet they thought twice before making the same mistake again! We always look forward to hearing these stories over dinner and discussing the success, or otherwise, of the day's teaching. A good day was one in which, "nobody fell off and nobody cried." I now use the same method when deciding how good my day's teaching has been! That is one of the many, many things I have taken from my time with Jen.

In this book, you will find insights, tips, skills and exercises that will help you in your quest for show jumping success. They are written with Jen's trademark clarity, style and focus on the techniques and details which I have found to be so crucial to my career in the sport. I know you will enjoy it.

Clarke Johnstone

 Every time you ride, you are teaching the horse to listen to you or teaching it to ignore you.

Jen Marsden Hamilton. Photo credit: Cheleken Photography.

When was the last time you practiced stride control?
Answer: The last time I rode! Make sure it isn't a lie.

Jen Marsden Hamilton. Photo credit: Alex Petersen.

Introduction

Sport Requires Passion

The great thing about sport is that it enables us to care passionately about something that really doesn't matter!

Scott Taylor
Winnipeg Free Press, 1987.

Sport is an emotional phenomenon that often combines tremendous status, important relationships, and winning and losing in a public forum where it is usually very difficult to conceal how well or poorly you've performed. To be good at sport demands tremendous psychological and physical skill.

Some of the most intense competitors in sport and life have the insight to occasionally remind themselves that sport is only a game, a recreation. Emotion gives life meaning and is what makes us human. It enhances our potential in more ways than we realize. It can fuel our lives, drive us crazy or break our hearts. Passion can ignite potential in a wide range of human performance fields including sport, business, teaching, parenting and the performing arts. Our passion energizes and motivates us. By developing our passion we can achieve our true potential.

Why does riding inspire passion, perhaps more than many other sport and hobby?

- There is a dedication threshold — once you cross it you are heavily committed by the sheer amount of time and money that is required.
- There is a unique mix of adrenalin, competitive spirit and variety each day — new challenges due to changing weather conditions and the horse's frame of mind.
- There is the concept of *bonding with a noble creature*. The trust and empathy you get from partnering with a powerful and kind creature. (Have you tried looking into the solemn brown eye of a running shoe?)
- There is the growth of technical knowledge that never ends: "The more you know, the more you realize how little you know."
- There is the fact that every horse is an individual who can teach you something about yourself as well as your training techniques (it is difficult to say the same of a bicycle).

Passion is the link to achieving your true potential. Through sport, you can grow as a person only if you recognize what it offers you.

Over the last 20 years I've traveled to many places to teach clinics, coach at horse shows, look at horses to buy and spectate at competitions of the highest level. I've been to New Zealand and Australia, Kenya, Columbia, Costa Rica, Guatemala, and Ecuador. I've been to Europe, India and across the United States and Canada. I have spent hours watching horses and riders. It's my passion.

My most interesting and memorable horse-related trip started with a phone call at three o'clock in the morning. I traveled to India to teach one very wealthy seventeen-year-old boy. I was to teach him to jump. It was to be a huge challenge because the first day of training the horses wouldn't even go near a pole on the ground, much less step over it. We persisted and eventually the boy was able to jump a simple 3ft course.

Balance, rhythm, straightness and pace were the foundation of any success we achieved. Everyday we worked on basic equitation, position and riding forward and straight. Stride control exercises between poles and jumps were practiced every day: "Do the line in five strides. Now a steady six. Now a forward four."

Some days the boy was quite good and other days he was not so good. On one particular day, the boy was awful. I said, "You have three tools to help you ride down the line properly: your eyes (and while I'm saying this I'm thinking to myself he rides like a blind man); the feeling of the stride (I'm thinking that one is not going to happen); and the counting of the strides — half way down the line you should be half way through the strides."

"Are you counting the strides?" I asked. "No!" he said, "you count them for me!" "Yeah..." I replied, "but what happens when I'm not here?" The boy turned in his saddle and pointed: "My man will count for me!"

That boy just didn't get it. That boy just didn't have the passion. What he considered boring and of little importance, we — the passionate people — consider essential, challenging, exciting and fun. That boy will probably never master the simple exercises and he won't progress. He lacked passion and will never be a true winner!

There are different outlets for passion in equestrian sports, such as schooling, teaching, competing, breeding and officiating.

Some people can train all their lives without competing and get total satisfaction from creating harmony, balance and a partnership with their horse. Teaching and coaching are about passing knowledge on. The love for the horse and our sport is what compels some of us to teach, and there is a clear distinction between teaching to make a difference and coaching for the money. It's that passion thing again!

A show jumping round is all over in a matter of minutes but riders are always thinking of the next class and dreaming of the next show. There is a compulsion and passion to get it right the next time.

For breeders, there is the whole mysterious mix of nature, nurture, genetics and education. It's this mystery that inspires passion in breeders.

For the show organizer, judge, course designer, steward or in-gate attendant who spend countless hours behind the scenes at horse shows, there has to be passion.

I've coached hundreds of riders and watched countless horses jump over coloured sticks. I've schooled some Olympic riders and helped to school horses that competed in the Olympic Games and at World Championships. It's my passion.

The equestrian skill-base and attitude which can take you on lovely hacks, galloping down a beach, hunting, competing at local shows and all the way to the Olympics, are developed from your first learning session at home. The skills and attitude you develop here and now are what will carry you through your life.

It isn't where you're from that's important. What's important is who you are. Channel the passion that you learn at home with a strong work ethic, a belief in yourself, hours of sweat and equestrian correctness into a positive passion and it will lead you to success and fun...

Dare to be a winner!

Scott Taylor from the Winnipeg Free Press is wrong when he says "The great thing about sport is that it enables us to care passionately about something that really doesn't matter!" Riding matters to us! Riding plays an integral part in helping us develop into the people we are and shapes our journey.

By developing your passion, riding and mental skills you can begin to achieve your true potential. Think of how and where you can ignite more passion to perform and raise your level of knowledge and success.

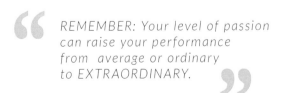

REMEMBER: Your level of passion can raise your performance from average or ordinary to EXTRAORDINARY.

Alex de Luca Oliveira and Clifton Checkers representing New Zealand at the World Equestrian Games 2006. Photo credit: WEG Aachen 2006.

ALEX DE LUCA New Zealand

The best thing about Jen is that she tells you what you need to know, not necessarily what you want to hear.

Alex "The Brazilian," riding for New Zealand on a New Zealand horse, trained by the Canadian.

Suzie Hayward and Andretti. Photo credit: Christine Cornege. Cornege Photography.

SUZIE HAYWARD New Zealand

I have a fabulous horse, Andretti. Jen's teaching is putting the basics into practice and riding correctly, with purpose. Her jumping exercises are great, her teaching of stride control is so important and logical to our sport.

> *When you are on a great horse, you have the best seat you will ever have.*
>
> Sir Winston Churchill.

Chapter 1
Training and Coaching

Mary Wakeman and MJ Lubeck. Photo credit: Show Circuit Magazine.

MARY WAKEMAN New Zealand

Jen's great training ability not only helps develop the horse's jump, but also the rider's confidence.

Success comes from the pursuit of excellence.

TRAINING AND COACHING

The chapters in this book are a progression of training exercises directed toward developing a training program which will turn untrained skills into mastered skills and strengths.

The riders I teach often hear me talk about responsibility. I am a great believer in taking responsibility for actions and performances. "If you want the glory of winning" I say, "take the responsibility for the ride!"

Responsibility: The Ability to Respond Correctly

It is only after reading Jeanette Wilson's book *Medium Rare* that I started to understand what I was saying. Wilson breaks the word "responsibility" down, and says taking responsibility for actions and performances is really the ability to respond correctly to a situation.

Question: How do we learn to respond correctly?
Answer: By having prior knowledge.

Training teaches new skills, refines and maintains learned skills, and helps to develop the ability to read a situation and problem-solve appropriately.

Humans gain prior knowledge through reading, directed problem-solving and by watching others act and deal with a situation.

Gaining knowledge in any sport is based on systematic skill progression. The most basic skills are taught first to form the foundation from which more advanced and intricate skills can be developed — one at a time.

This Book

In this book, I have identified the fundamental skills that I consider essential. These start with correct rider position and application of the aids, as well as learning to use the different rein aids to ride correct, accurate turns.

Stride control (striding) is an essential part for improving rideability and allows us to further improve the horse's technique.

Each chapter has been broken down into exercises specifically designed to teach each skill.

Once you learn a new skill, it is your responsibility to practice it over and over again until its execution becomes automatic. A new skill becomes a mastered skill once it becomes a habit.

Riding is a non-verbal activity. If the horse understood English, I could tell him what to do and we wouldn't need you.

'Okay coach... I've got it – Eyes, position and leg!'

Illustration by my dear friend Tisha Pratt.

The Importance of Having a Coach

I think it is very important for all riders, regardless of how novice or elite their level, to have a coach. Coaches are a major ingredient in helping riders learn responsibility. Training on your own can train bad habits. In order to respond correctly, especially under pressure, the rider must have good habits to de-clutter their brain and narrow the focus in competition.

Coaches are the eyes on the ground, they can see the whole picture and help direct learning. They can analyze the influence the rider has on the horse, and can teach and confirm positional corrections and technique, as well as be involved in decision-making.

I am a believer in national coaching programs. Coaching programs really don't teach specific sport skills. The programs help establish teaching and coaching skills.

Educated coaches produce educated riders. They promote correct riding technique until they become ingrained habits. A coach who understands and can teach the skills required can develop a strong foundation in riders from which further progress can be made.

Trained coaches identify the skill required and give exercises that teach the skill.

Coaches teach new skills one at a time, rather than overwhelm their students with too many skills and they teach these at the slowest pace possible. For example, when teaching a crest or jumping release, they have the rider practice it while standing still. Once the rider has the feel of it, they try it at a walk, trot, canter and, finally, over a jump.

Good and responsible coaching and training develops a sound foundation of basics based on:

- Balance
- Rhythm
- Straightness
- Pace

> *That wasn't really a transition... You just stopped cantering.*

> *Half way through the line, you should be half way through the count...*

Jen Marsden Hamilton. Photo credits: Alex Petersen.

> *Coaches should teach independent problem solving, not reliance.*

> *Do it right the first time!*

> *Training should teach correctness and how to problem solve; how to take responsibility.*

Jen Marsden Hamilton. Photo credit: Alex Petersen.

Riding Versus Coaching

It is important to understand the difference between riding and coaching. The two skill areas require different talents for communication. The rider uses non-verbal and intuitive skills, whereas the coach uses verbal and analytical skills.

The rider possesses a rapid, complex, non-verbal communication with their horse, an instinctive and/or intuitive communication in the case of a truly talented rider. The rider has no need to intellectualize or verbalize their actions.

A winning rider is not necessarily a winning coach. It is the exceptional individual who possesses the ability to excel at both riding and coaching. A knowledge found through intuition or instinct can be difficult to communicate with depth or intelligence to a student.

The coach's communication with his students is analytical and verbal. Coaches must understand the actions necessary for a performance and communicate them verbally to their students. Not only must the coach communicate, they must do so with clarity, in order for the student to fully understand.

To be a winning rider and coach, the person must have the ability not only to ride, but also to be able to analyze actions and communicate these actions verbally.

**The most important thing in training, riding and coaching is:
Don't skip the basics! Don't over drill!**

Chris Hadfield is one of my heroes. He is a Canadian astronaut who commanded the International Space Station. He also believes in taking responsibility for actions, and trained hard to understand and respond correctly to situations that presented themselves. Chris Hadfield is a practicer. He practiced skills over and over until they were habits. He thought of all the bad things that could happen and developed strategies for top performance. Chris Hadfield had to take responsibility for his own actions and for the lives of others.

Remember that every time you ride, you are forming habits — good habits or bad habits. You might as well form good habits!

Every time you ride, you should ride to the best of your ability, you should practice correctness and good habits. Pay attention to the details. Every line, turn or transition you ride should be the best one of your life. Form good habits and train your horse to be correct, supple and obedient.

The chapters in this book have been based on my own training and education, riding and competing experiences, professional training in equestrian coaching and personal coaching experiences. Riders and owners come to me for coaching because of my track record of producing knowledgeable, educated riders and horses, as well as riders who perform and compete comfortably and confidently with positive results.

I am a trained teacher and coach. I am passionate about teaching the verbal communication of knowledge to others. I also believe that coaching should teach and not just show people how to compete. Correct teaching lasts a lifetime.

Training should teach correctness and how to problem solve; how to take responsibility.

As Chris Hadfield says, "Train with passion so you can be prepared just in case!" Enjoy training, so you can be a winner and take responsibility for the ride!

Winning is not just achieving a first placing. It is defined by riding to the best of your ability, training, and competing hard and correctly. Success breeds success and, if you keep improving your performance, you are doing something right. Keep training with correctness and you'll become a winner and when you finally hold up the trophy, you will actually deserve it!

There is no magic wand or big secret to winning. It takes hours and hours of correct training, the internalizing of skills and techniques, the desire to win, strategic competition plans, as well as the right horse.

Help yourself and your horse to become the best athletes possible.

David Colette and Buster. Photo credit: Angie Ivory.

Horses teach us more than just about riding.
They teach us so much about ourselves.

Maddy Fleming (Age 9) and Dream Works. Photo Credit: Jensen Shoebridge.

MADDY FLEMING Nova Scotia, Canada

She makes me feel brave and confident, especially when she yells "Use your eyes! Use your legs!"

I do not yell! I speak with passion.

Jen Marsden Hamilton. Photo credit: Cheleken Photography.

Chapter 2
Back to Basics
Position and Rein Aids

Stevie Murphy (Age 12) and Austin at the Royal Winter Fair, Champion Canadian Large Pony, 2006. Photo credit: S. Murphy.

STEVIE MURPHY Prince Edward Island, Canada

Jen built my foundation as a rider, while showing me the results that hard work, practice, dedication, and preparation can have within one's riding career. Austin and I went from Austin stopping and me falling off, to being champions!

Never let go of a stopper with your leg or your hand.

CREATING GOOD HABITS

Every time you ride you should ride to the best of your ability, practice correctness and establish good habits. Habits are the foundation of your riding and you want to build a good, strong and correct foundation. Correct habits de-clutter the brain, so the "here and now" are the main focus.

When you are on course there is no time to think. There is only time to assess, correct and ride the strategy.

All of the techniques I teach have to become habits so you don't have to think about them.

If you have to think about going straight after a jump and not cutting corners or you have to remember to keep your elbows bent or your heels down and in, you haven't done enough homework and training to be in the competition ring.

CORRECT POSITION

A correct basic position is not about making the rider look pretty — it is about making the rider functional. A correct position allows a correct and safe jump and a faulty position almost guarantees a bad jump!

Three-Point Position

The basic position is called the three-point position. The three points being, the seat and two legs that form the rider's base of support. In this position, the head, shoulder, hip and heel are in line. About two-thirds of the rider's weight is in the seat and there is a straight line from the rider's elbow to the horse's mouth.

The Rider's Seat and Leg

The seat is the rider's centre of gravity. The rider sits in the saddle as close to the pommel as possible. The thighs are forward and in. The knees are relaxed. Stirrup is on the ball of the foot. The lower leg is the base of support and is controlled by keeping the heel down, back and in.

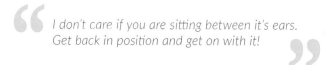

I don't care if you are sitting between it's ears.
Get back in position and get on with it!

Legs are used for:
- Base of support, they hold you on.
- Longitudinal control and lateral control — creates straightness.
- Impulsion and power.

In three-point, the base of support is the seat and rider's two legs. The function of the legs is to apply clear aids for longitudinal work, lateral work, creating impulsion or power.

Three-Point Position

- Seat and two legs are your base of support.
- Head, shoulder, hip and heel are in line.
- Sit close to the pommel.
- Thighs forward and in.
- Knees relaxed.
- Stirrup on the ball of foot.

- Lower leg is controlled by keeping the heel down, back and in.
- Back is stretched, flat and relaxed.
- Hands held over and in front of the withers, almost touching.
- Straight wrists, hands on 45 degree angle, elbows bent.
- Eyes give balance, direction and allow rider to feel.

Three-point position is flatwork position.

Jennifer Sarsfield and Ozaria. Photo credit: Carolyn Hazel.

If the lower leg is too far forward, it will place the rider behind the motion and the rider will get left behind over the jump. If the lower leg is too far back, it will place the rider ahead of the motion, causing the rider to jump up the horse's neck at the take off of the jump.

Never kick the horse at the base of the jump. In order to kick you have to take your leg off first, abandoning your position and your "go button!"

The Rider's Back

The rider's back is stretched up, flat and relaxed. A back that is too arched creates stiffness in the arms and a roach back is weak and ineffective.

An arched back ("the perch") creates stiff arms and a stiff ride. The rider does not stay in rhythm with the horse and often loses position at the jump.

A roach back is weak and ineffective.

Jennifer Sarsfield and Ozaria. Photo credit: Carolyn Hazel.

The Rider's Arms and Hands

The arms and hands follow the motion of the horse. The hands are held over and in front of the withers, with flat/straight wrists and on a 45 degree angle, almost touching.

There should be a straight line from the rider's elbow to the bit. When we talk about softness of the hand, really we are talking about softness of the elbow. The hands are to be :

- Straight
- Steady
- Definite
- Supple
- Giving

Jennifer Sarsfield and Ozaria.
Photo credit: Carolyn Hazel.

The Rider's Eyes

- Give balance
- Direction
- Allow the rider to feel
- Look where you want to go. When you are looking down, you are half way to falling off.
- If you are looking, you might find the distance!

Craig Sullivan and Centre Stage. Photo credit: Angie Ivory.

Two-Point Position

Two-point is the jumping position. It puts the rider in motion with the horse. The seat is raised out of the saddle and the rider's hip angle is closed. In two-point position, the rider's two legs are the base of support. But, if in trouble sink down, shoulders back, and use eyes for balance and direction. Get slightly behind the horse and ride forward.

- Legs are the base of support.
- Seat is raised and hip angle is closed.
- Thighs forward and in.
- Stirrup on ball of foot.
- Lower leg is controlled by keeping the heel down, back and in.

- Back is stretched, flat, relaxed.
- Hands held over and in front of the withers.
- Straight wrists, hands on 45 degree angle, elbows bent.
- Eyes give balance, direction and allow rider to feel.

Two-point position. The rider's base of support is the two legs. Jennifer Sarsfield and Ozaria. Photo credit: Carolyn Hazel.

KEY POINTS ▬ ▬ ▬ ▬ ▬ ▬ ▬ ▬ ▬

Never skip the basics. The basics start with correct rider position.

Three-point is flatwork position. Transitions are done in three-point. Position, then the transition.

Two-point is jumping position.

The more trouble you're in, the better your position has to become. Position can save lives!

REIN AIDS

Rein aids are used to communicate with your horse. If you want the horse to back up, that's different from wanting to turn, so you have different rein aids for different responses.

Your hands are to be held over and in front of the withers because the force of your rein should go in a straight line from the bit through your hip line — that's where the physics are correct and you can connect with the horse's mouth properly. If you drop your hand, you end up altering your position and the mechanics of your rein aids are all wrong.

The hands control from the withers forward. The leg controls from the withers back.

1. Direct Rein

The first rein aid is the direct rein. The force of the rein goes directly back towards your hip on the same side. The direct rein directs the horse's weight from the forehand to the hind end. Direct reins control pace and balance. You ride forward from your leg into contact and contact is direct pressure. Contact is balance. Leg to hand creates connection and directs the horse's weight to the hind end, lightening the front end.

Direct rein. Controls pace and balance. Karen Lyon and Lyon Lodge Kinder Surprise. Photo credit: Horses and People Magazine.

2. Indirect Rein

An indirect rein directs the force of the rein toward the rider's opposite hip. An indirect rein in front of the withers transfers the horse's balance from one shoulder to the other. An indirect rein behind the withers directs the horse's balance from the shoulder to the opposite hip and hock. Indirect reins create bend. Softening the horse laterally by bending creates a softer horse longitudinally.

Indirect rein behind the withers. Photo credit: Horses and People Magazine.

3. Bearing Rein / Neck Rein

The bearing rein presses into the neck in front of the wither. The bearing rein stops sideways motion. The more you pull a horse with one rein around a turn, the more it will drift sideways. Use a bearing rein to block sideways motion. It stops the "rubber-necking."

4. Open Rein / Leading Rein

The rider's hand and rein open away from the horse's neck at the level of the other hand. It only goes out as far as the rider's hip. An open rein fine tunes the track and does not disturb the forward motion.

Extending the open rein becomes a leading rein — used mostly on young horses. It's also used on jumpers for very tight turns because it does not disturb pace.

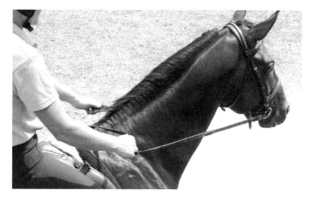

Right open rein. The outside (left) hand becomes a bearing rein to correct any drift or side motion. Photo credit: Horses and People Magazine.

5. Pulley Rein

The pulley rein is your emergency stop. It is also used by eventers on cross country when entering the zone of the jump from the gallop. Put your fist into the neck, brace with it and pull the horse up with the other rein.

Pulley rein. Photo credit: Horses and People Magazine.

KEY POINTS ▬ ▬ ▬ ▬ ▬ ▬ ▬ ▬

Riding is about creating energy from leg to hand to create a connection (a package of energy). This connection from back to front and held side to side produces rhythm, pace, direction, and shape (straight or bend). The coordination of leg and rein aids communicates with the horse in a simple, clear and productive way.

Horses can only perform to the level of communication from the rider. The use of rein aids in conjunction with the leg, helps clarify communication.

Anna Douglass and Young Pretender. Photo credit: Rosa Douglass.

ANNA DOUGLASS New Zealand

Jen believes a tan makes her look thinner. Jen always reminds me of one particular time when I got dressed for my lesson the night before — sleeping in my jodhpurs and getting straight out of bed the next morning, quickly saddling my horse in the dark and beating Jen out to the arena!

> *Punctuality is a sign of respect. And respect goes in both directions!*

Chapter 3
Putting Theory into Practice

Kim Durling and Zadinus. Photo credit: MLM photography.

KIM DURLING Nova Scotia, Canada

With Jen's help I can ride into the ring with conviction and knowledge that whatever the course designer has presented us with, my horse and I can conquer.

You are a problem solver, not a problem creator.

PUTTING THEORY INTO PRACTICE

When on course in competition there is no time to think, there is only time to assess the situation and make adjustments to follow the strategy. Thinking is done at home. Once the skill is a habit you don't have to focus on it (see Creating Good Habits on page 32).

You walk the show jumping course to build a strategy. It is your responsibility as a rider to ride the track and setup the stride/pace on the short side of the arena for what's required in the line of jumps.

God made the horse under the Imperial System and God said the horse shall have a 12ft stride. At least in North America! Courses and related lines are based on the 12ft stride. A 60ft line of jumps will ride as four 12ft strides (taking into account that one of those 12ft increments counts as the space required for landing and take off).

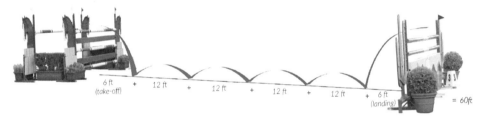

| 6 ft (take-off) | + | 12 ft | + | 12 ft | + | 12 ft | + | 12 ft | + | 6 ft (landing) | = 60ft |

In order to get around lower level courses, you need three different canters: regular canter (middle), open and closed canters.

It is the rider's responsibility to set and maintain stride length and pace. All lines do not ride the same and riders and horses need to learn and like jumping off different stride lengths.

Factors to be considered when setting stride (pace):

- Actual measurement between jumps— distance long, short or lovely.
- Types of jumps — vertical to oxer, oxer to vertical, vertical to vertical, etc.
- Where the line is on course — first or last.
- How close the jump is to the turn — the jump takes away pace combined with a short turn.
- Towards or away from the in-gate.
- Distractions.

EXERCISE 1: 60FT LINE OF GROUND POLES

For this exercise you need two poles 60ft apart along the long side of the arena.

Use a tape measure and measure from both ends of the poles to ensure they are parallel and the right distance apart. It also pays to mark the position of the poles with cones or a pair of jump wings. This way you will notice if the horse knocks a pole and alters the distance.

Stride control between the pole is longitudinal work (back to front). Serpentines and turn on the forehand are lateral work (side to side).

- Canter the poles in five strides — this is your middle canter.
- Ride a serpentine of three loops — canter the first loop, trot the second loop, canter the third loop, making your transitions on the centre line.
- Halt on the centre line and turn on the forehand to change the rein.
- Canter around the arena and canter the poles in five strides again.
- Ride a serpentine of three loops — trot the first loop, canter the second loop, trot the third loop.
- Walk on the centre line.

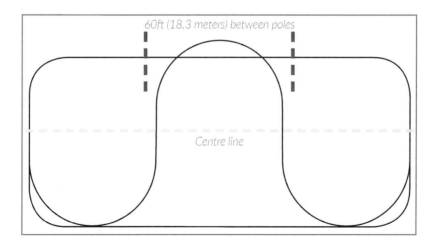

Exercise 1: Purpose

- To teach the rider to take responsibility for setting up, on the short side of the arena, the stride length required in the line which is determined by the distance between the poles (longitudinal work).

- To teach the rider to organize and turn, straighten and turn as they ride the serpentine (lateral work).

- The transitions teach both rider and horse discipline and accuracy (longitudinal work).

- The turn on the forehand teaches the rider coordination of aids and the horse to yield or move off the pressure of one leg aid (lateral work).

- Cantering down the long side may seem like an empty task; it isn't. The transition to trot on the centre line, the start of the serpentine, teaches the rider to think and organize.

- A downward transition to walk on the centre line on completion of the serpentine finishes the ride neatly.

Further Education

The short sides of the arena are an important part of the course. This is where the organization is done. It is on the short side that the rider prepares the horse for what's coming. The horse doesn't know the course and distances. The rider does and this mental knowledge has to be turned into physical action.

There are two parts of the short side: the setup and recovery.

The Setup Time

The distance from the centre line to the first pole or jump of the line is the minimum setup time. This is where pace is established for what is required to get down the line.

The Recovery Time

AWAY FROM ONE JUMP IS TO THE NEXT! The recovery time is where you have to fix any loss of position, connection, balance, shape, lead, pace and track.

The distance from your last jump to the centre line of your turn, on a lovely perpendicular, parallel path (because we never cut corners), is your recovery time. It's your maximum recovery time.

When the setup and recovery are put together — recovery time leads to setup time. Ideally, you want to reduce the recovery time to give more setup time. This is done by riding straight away from the last jump of the line on a perpendicular straight track to the turn. Hopefully, position, balance, pace, and lead are maintained or corrected at the turn and the recovery is completed early. This gives more of the short side to the setup for the next line.

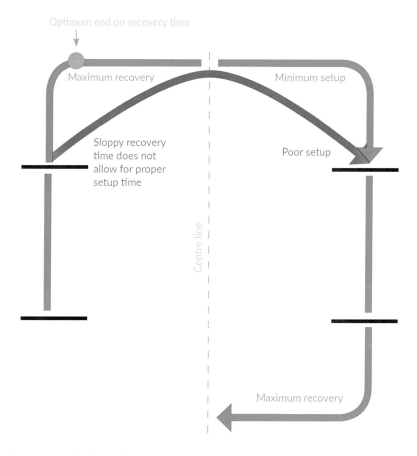

Show jumping ring illustrating setup and recovery.

RIDING THE SETUP TIME

On the short side of the arena, the balance and pace are established (longitudinal connection). Through the turn, the horse will tend to bulge or drift to the outside.

Ride from outside to inside.

Use an inside open rein and an outside bearing rein with direct pressure, and an outside leg to guide the horse around the turn. The outside leg and outside bearing rein block any potential drift and maintain balance. Pace is maintained with the inside leg. The open rein won't disturb the established pace. The hands are moved to the inside of the arc being ridden. As the turn is being completed, the hands return to the neutral position and the horse is straightened and balanced with an outside direct rein. You do not want the horse bent through this turn because it will shorten the stride and the horse will get crooked.

Ride the line.

RIDING THE RECOVERY TIME

As the horse lands off the last pole or jump of the line use direct reins to re-balance. Look straight to go straight — follow your eyes to see the turn and give yourself direction.

Ride from inside to outside.

Riders tend to let horses cut corners and fall in going into turns. Use your inside leg to push to the outside rein and leg. Direct pressure on the outside rein will help control balance and pace as the rein opens to guide the horse straight. The inside indirect rein and inside leg are used to bend and shape the horse for the turn. The outside rein will control pace, balance, amount of bend and holds the track. The hands move to the outside of the arc being ridden and then return to their neutral position and even contact.

The habit of riding the recovery time smoothly and accurately enables a smooth and definite setup time. The better the turn the better the line.

THE BETTER THE TURN, THE BETTER THE LINE

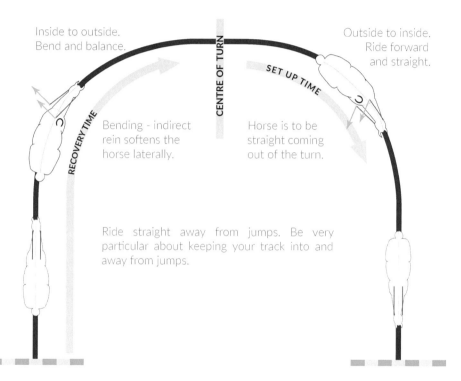

Inside to outside.
Bend and balance.

CENTRE OF TURN

SET UP TIME

Outside to inside.
Ride forward
and straight.

RECOVERY TIME

Bending - indirect
rein softens the
horse laterally.

Horse is to be
straight coming
out of the turn.

Ride straight away from jumps. Be very
particular about keeping your track into and
away from jumps.

EXERCISE 2: INCREASING RIDEABILITY

- Canter the 60ft poles in 5 strides.
- Serpentine of three loops — canter the first loop, trot the second, canter the third. Ride the transitions accurately on the centre line with a straight horse.
- Canter over the poles in the forward (open or longer) 4 strides.
- Continue around the arena and ride two canter-walk-canter transitions.
- Canter the poles in the steady (closed or shorter) 6 strides.
- Serpentine of three loops with either flying or simple changes.
- Canter the poles in 5 strides.
- Finish the exercise neatly with a transition to the walk.

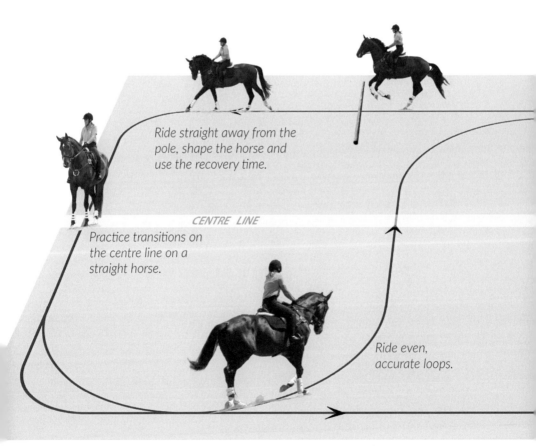

Ride straight away from the pole, shape the horse and use the recovery time.

CENTRE LINE

Practice transitions on the centre line on a straight horse.

Ride even, accurate loops.

In the second exercise, canter the line in the middle five, the open four, the steady six and again in the middle five.

Exercise 2: Purpose

This exercise builds on the first one practiced by having to ride the line in the three different canters. Establish the three different stride lengths on the short side. A correct use of the recovery time gives the space and time to setup for the next task.

Developing feel for the different canters, riding with leg to hand connection, combined with the correct use of the rein aids, improves the approach to the jump and, therefore, improves the jump.

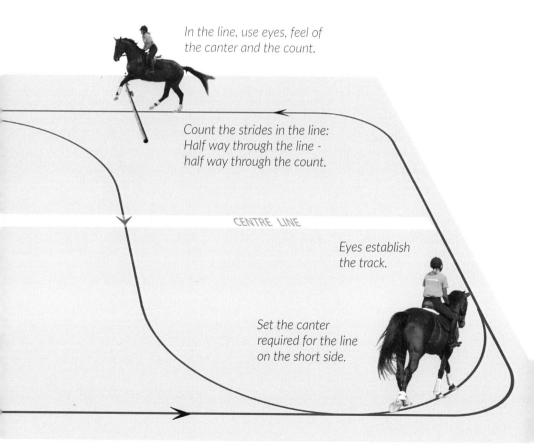

In the line, use eyes, feel of the canter and the count.

Count the strides in the line: Half way through the line - half way through the count.

CENTRE LINE

Eyes establish the track.

Set the canter required for the line on the short side.

Stride control exercises teach riders to take responsibility for developing the horse's rideability. First, the rider needs to know and have the feel for different strides.

- How do you develop feel? With stride control exercises.
- How do you teach horses to go forward and come back? Using your leg and rein aids.
- How do you improve the ride down the line? You improve the turn.

Horses are not like cars. They don't have a cruise control button. The rider has to know when to press the accelerator and when to apply the brakes. It sounds so easy to say: "Set the stride on the short side and the line will take care of itself." It's a great theory but riders have to ride reality.

Training is about correct practice to develop good habits. Practice setting the pace on the short side to the best of your ability based on feel. Once in the line read the situation. Count the strides. Half way down the line you should be half way through the count. To make the ride happen you have three options: move up (lengthen the stride), steady (shorten the stride) or keep what you've got.

Ideally, if your setup was correct you can keep the canter you have. If you see, feel, and count that you are getting there too soon — shoulders back and use direct reins — steady. If you see, feel and count that you are weak — shoulders back and leg — move up. If you see, feel, and count that all is good — keep what you've got.

If you "miss" and, for example, put in 6 strides when you wanted 5, learn from the mistake and do a better setup next time or do a better job controlling the stride within the line and make the correction in the recovery time. Training is when you learn from mistakes and take responsibility for improving performance.

Don't become the queen of the perfect mistake!

Correct Practice

Correct training and good habits come from paying attention to the details, and internalizing the skills required to get the correct response.

A correct position that allows you to deliver clear and precise aids is the most important thing in riding. Make it a habit. Every transition, circle, serpentine, turn, etc., should be done to the best of your ability. Every time you ride down a line, read the situation and maintain or adjust the pace, balance and straightness as required. Educate yourself and your horse.

Consistency leads to good habits, improves discipline and communication which raises the level of performance and makes you a winner!

KEY POINTS ▬ ▬ ▬ ▬ ▬ ▬ ▬ ▬

You have eyes for balance, direction, distance and conviction. Your eyes create the final conviction that you want to jump the jump. Use them and you might see that *elusive distance*.

A successful course ride is a combination of rider-horse communication. Through stride control exercises, the rider learns how to produce and feel stride, and the horse learns to listen and respect the rider.

Effective use of the short side changes a frantic ride into an educated ride.

Horses and People met along the way

1. Rosalind James Laperriere and Spoil Sport. Photo credit: Helen Snow.

2. Kathy Woolaver and Ermentrude. Photo credit: B. Woolaver.

3. Brian and Jen Marsden Hamilton and Loctite. Winner of the Oland's Stake at The Atlantic Winter Fair, 1972. Photo credit: AWF.

4. Victoria Andrew and The Who. Photo credit: Prezyna Art & Photography.

5. Valerie Phelan and Amenia. Photo credit: Megan Touchie.

6. Annabel Bleicher and Megan Hamilton and Stormy. Photo credit: Francis Doucette.

7. Sarah Burns Swanson and Equador. Hunter to Jumper in one day. Photo credit: Helen Snow.

4

5

6

7

7

" Hunter to Jumper in one day. Just change the tack! "

Horses and People met along the way

1. Marilyn Miller and Graphic Art. Photo credit: Helen Snow.

2. Gail Morash Shea and Quiet Company. Photo credit: Helen Snow.

3. Deanna and Valerie Phelan. Photo credit: Kate Burke.

4. Sandra Konok Wilson and Risky Business. Photo credit: H. Konok.

5. Megan Hamilton Lorius riding for Canada in Guatemala. Photo credit: Jen Marsden Hamilton.

6. Annabel Bleicher and Emma of Normandy. Photo credit: Barbie Caldwell.

7. Megan Hamilton Lorius and Private Benjamin. Photo credit: Jen Marsden Hamilton.

8. Christopher Hamilton and AJ. Photo credit: Jen Marsden Hamilton.

Fashion may change but good riding is good riding.

Horses and People met along the way

1. Liz Hardy and Castle's Gold.
Photo credit: Andrea Hardy.

2. Tisha Pratt and Tess.
Photo credit: Denya.

3. Cristina Wilkins and Luisillo.
Editor of Horses and People
Magazine. Photo credit:
Linda Zupanc.

4. Alex George Beaton and
Alderman. Photo credit:
Deirdre George.

5. Veronica Waddy and Milburn
Melody. Photo credit: Barbara
Thomson Photography.

6. Davina Waddy and Milburn
Marino. Photo credit: Annie
Studholme Equine Photography.

7. Cristina Wilkins and Luisillo.
Photo credit: Nicholas Wilkins.

8. Karen Lyon and Lyon Lodge
Kinder Surprise. Photo Credit:
Horses and People Magazine.

1

2

3

4

5

6

7

8

5

6

7

1. Kathleen Youden and Fun to Fly. Photo credit: Michelle MacKenzy MLM Photography.

2. Kathleen Youden and Pravda. Photo credit: Kathleen Youden.

3. Nikki Meyer and Conquistador. Photo credit: Michel Bellerive.

4. Nathalie Green and Fritz. Photo credit: Kenneth Jollymore.

5. Jennifer Sarsfiled and Ozaria. Photo credit: Victoria Clermont.

6. Jill Swain and Fiarmo. Photo credit: Tom Von Kapherr.

7. Craig Sullivan and Center Stage. Photo credit: Angie Ivory.

Sharon Meek and Dingo Creek at the New Zealand Horse of The Year 2009, New Zealand Amateur Rider of The Year class. 1-10m to 1-20m. Photo credit: Barbara Thomson Photography.

SHARON MEEK New Zealand

I was 58 years old and Dingo Creek was an 11-year-old, 15.1 hh, Quarter Horse cross gelding. Never had I jumped 1.20m but, with Jen Hamilton's coaching of self-belief and dedicated training, I achieved my goal, which was to compete in the New Zealand Amateur Rider of the Year class.

You are never too old to learn and improve! And you have proven this to be true.

Chapter 4

Rideability

Grace Manera and Tallyho Neptune. Pony Grand Prix 1.25m. 2nd place.
Photo credit: Maria Townsend.

GRACE MANERA New Zealand

Grace has been training with Jen since she was on a 12.2hh pony. Jen's knowledge is immense and the confidence she gives the children is amazing.

" This beautiful picture gives the illusion of flying. The rider and pony are one. I can almost see the wings on the pony. "

TAKING RESPONSIBILITY FOR THE RIDE

The most difficult part of jumping a course is getting to the jumps and that is flat work.

Courses are designed so that different lines require different stride lengths and take-off points.

The rider has the knowledge of what is coming up (the course plan and related distances), not the horse. The horse doesn't walk the course, the rider does.

Based on the course walk, the rider builds a course strategy. When on course, the mental knowledge must be turned into physical action.

Stride control exercises are one aspect of training jumpers. They are used to make both horse and rider comfortable with the different tests course designers set to challenge us — forward distances, short distances, long runs to individual jumps, etc.

Horses have to be trained to be rideable, trained to develop a range and elasticity of different strides, and produce these on demand.

In this chapter we build on stride control exercises by moving from ground poles to jumps, and introduce a new pole exercise to increase rideability and give you and your horse more options on course.

EXERCISE 1: STRIDE CONTROL OVER JUMPS

For this first exercise, you need to build two jumps — a vertical and an oxer — 60ft apart (18.30 meters) on the long side of the arena.

This is the same 60ft distance covered in Chapter 2: Putting Theory Into Practice. All you need to do is add some jump standards and ground poles.

Use a tape measure and remember the distance is measured inside the line — from the vertical to the first rail of the oxer. The height of the jumps depend on your own and your horse's level of experience. Start low and raise the height when you are confident that you are achieving the tasks required.

The purpose of this exercise is to teach rider and horse to:

- Jump from different take-off points (distances).
- Jump from different stride lengths at the first jump of the line (the vertical).

Exercises like this allow the rider to learn to read the situation — develop an "eye" and to efficiently use the setup and recovery areas as I described in the last chapter.

Exercise 1

- Trot into the first jump (vertical) and canter to the oxer in five strides.
- Serpentine of 3 loops — canter the first loop, trot the second loop and canter the third loop. Ride neat, accurate transitions on the centre line with a straight horse. Three-point position (flatwork).
- Canter the line in the true 4 strides. Two-point position.
- Canter around the arena doing 1 or 2 canter-walk-canter transitions along the long side of the arena. Three-point position.
- Canter the line in 5 steady strides (this means you are adding one stride in the line). Two-point position.
- Serpentine of 3 loops doing simple changes of lead (through walk) or flying changes of lead. Two or three-point position.
- Canter the line in the true 4 strides. Two-point position.
- Finish the exercise neatly, riding a straight and clean canter to walk transition on the centre line. Three-point position.

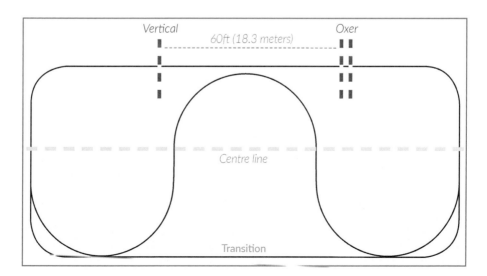

Exercise 1: Strategy

Trotting to the first jump teaches the horse to jump from a deep/close distance, to wait and develop a correct arc over the jump.

- Teaches the rider patience, a correct position, to go deep and like that distance, and it teaches both horse and rider bravery.

- Trotting to the first jump can make the line to the oxer ride slightly forward in the first few strides. This is because the canter is being established away from the first jump.

- The serpentine, with transitions, teaches discipline to both rider and horse.

- Cantering the line in 4 strides is based on a 12ft stride and this is "the true ride." Approaching in canter, the take-off point will be further out (more gap to the jump) than when jumping from the trot.

- The canter-walk-canter transitions are used as a preparation for closing or shortening the stride.

- Cantering the line in 5 strides requires a closed or shortened stride. The addition of a stride makes the horse jump from a closer distance than when riding the line in the 4 strides, and a bit further out than when trotting.

- The serpentine with either simple changes or flying changes teaches discipline and preparation. If the horse resisted in the closed 5 stride exercise, ride simple changes to improve the horse's response to the half halt "come back and wait" rein aids.

- If riding the line in 5 closed strides was easy and smooth, practice flying changes between the loops. Remember to keep the shape of the serpentine and the horse, as well as the balance through the changes of direction, within the serpentine. This is not a time to let the ride fall apart.

- Canter the line in the true 4 strides. This reinforces the true ride and the correct set-up on the short side.

If you don't plan on being a winner, don't even pick up the reins. If you want to be a winner, train hard and correctly — and then ride to be a winner.

Take Off Points

- Red: trot, deep.
- Green: True four.
- Blue: Steady five, closed stride.

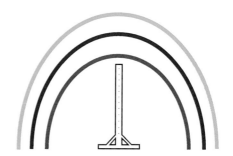

> *The stride that is added or subtracted in the line, is really added or subtracted through the turn.*

Developing your options

Training develops options. When riding to a jump, there are always three options:

- Move up (increase the stride): **going with** the forward distance that is seen.
- Steady (decrease the stride): **going against** the distance that is seen.
- Keep what you've got (maintain the stride): **going with** the distance seen.

These three options are always there, but that doesn't mean they are always appropriate!

Most riders have a preference for one of the three rides; some riders like to always move up, but this can teach the horse aggression or rushing. Others like to hold and steady, but this can create "chickens" (teaching your horse to stop).

Learning to use the short side of the arena (the recovery and setup phases) correctly, allows the rider to make decisions regarding stride length based on knowledge and confidence.

Commit yourself to the stride you've set up with conviction. If the line rode correctly, great. If it wasn't that great, change the turn the next time by altering the stride length.

If you make a mistake, learn from it and fix the ride. Don't practice mistakes until they are perfect mistakes! Develop the feel for three canters — the true 12ft stride, the closed stride and the open stride. Practice and learn to find the jump from the different canter strides.

Why? Because when you finally get to the jump, there's no such thing as a bad distance. That's where you are — love it! Support the ride with your leg, position and your conviction, using your eyes to keep looking for the track away.

These days, show jumping courses are technical and riders can no longer just ride "off their eye," or always jump from their preferred distance. It is the course designers who dictate how related lines should be ridden.

They do this through altering the distances between jumps, the types of jumps in the line and other factors. As a rider you have to train hard, long and correctly to meet these challenges.

During competition, it is essential to use the mental knowledge gained from the course walk to set up the ride on the short sides, so you can keep what you've got to the first jump of the line and then fine tune the canter in the line based on:

- your eye,
- the feel, and
- the count.

The option "keep what you've got," reduces the chances of confusion and will always produce a better jump. Horses do not appreciate riders who constantly change their minds in front of jumps, so keep what you've got and train your horse to jump from that distance.

Use the tools learned through stride control exercises and the use of the setup phase and recovery phase to give yourself more time to get organized, and set up an appropriate ride based on training and knowledge — not panic and desperation.

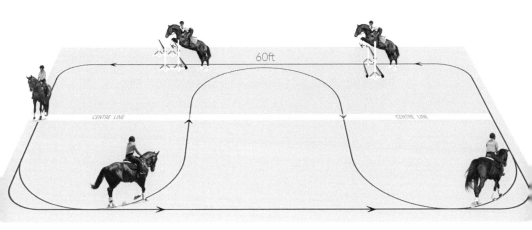

60ft

CENTRE LINE

CENTRE LINE

KEY POINTS ▬ ▬ ▬ ▬ ▬ ▬ ▬ ▬ ▬

Stride control exercises over jumps add the elements of needing "more correct pace and impulsion." The setup and recovery areas are taking on more importance.

There is no fine line to a perfect distance. Horses and riders have to learn and love to jump off different stride lengths and take off points.

Through stride control exercises, riders learn to read the situation, act accordingly and ride with conviction.

EXERCISE 2: INCREASING RIDEABILITY

I'm including this exercise over poles after the jumping exercise because to tell the truth, pole exercises can be more difficult. Exercises over poles teach many skills without wearing the legs off the horse.

Set up 3 ground poles 45ft apart (13.7m) from each other. Marking the exact placement of the poles with jump wings or cones will make it easier to check they stay in the right place.

This stride control exercise includes two related distances and the distance (45ft) dictates it is either a 3 stride distance or a steady 4 strides.

One related distance is quite easy to ride. Two related distances, one immediately after the other and on such a short distance, increases the challenge.

Exercise 2

- Set up the canter on the short side and canter down the line in two-point position.
- Count the strides between the first two poles — 45ft will ride as either 3 or 4 clean strides (not half strides).
- You must assess the canter (the length of stride, feel and count of strides) in the first part of the line, and reproduce it in the second part. What you do in the first part, do it in the second part.
- Ride a neat change of direction with a simple or flying change and canter down the line in the other direction. If the line was ridden in 4 to 4 (a closed stride) the first time, you will now ride it in 3 to 3 (a more open stride) on the return or vice versa.
- Ride a canter-walk transition on the centre line.

Exercise 2: Strategy

This exercise is much more difficult and will help you learn to setup and assess the canter, and make decisions based on feel.

Although the actual measurement between the poles is the same 45ft, the two parts won't necessarily ride the same. This means the rider will have to take more responsibility for the ride than when riding the previous exercise.

Exercise 2: Increasing Rideability

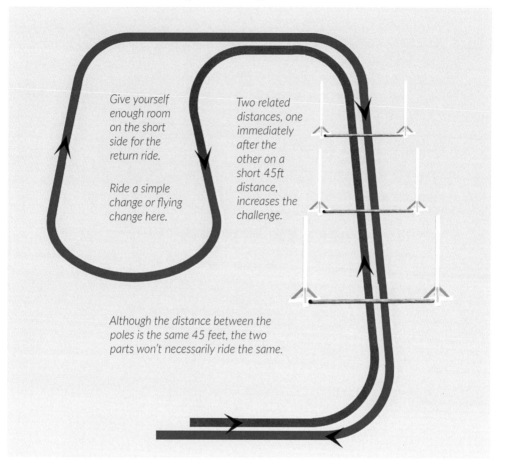

Give yourself enough room on the short side for the return ride.

Ride a simple change or flying change here.

Two related distances, one immediately after the other on a short 45ft distance, increases the challenge.

Although the distance between the poles is the same 45 feet, the two parts won't necessarily ride the same.

Exercises 2 and 3 track, showing an accurate track and neat changes of direction through the centre line.

KEY POINTS ▬ ▬ ▬ ▬ ▬ ▬ ▬ ▬

The 1st part of the exercise is the assessment and the second part is maintaining the stride.

- See
- Feel
- Count

- Feel and fix!

The first time you canter down the line, you should ride in a two-point position. It doesn't matter if you ride the line in 3 strides or 4 strides, as long as what you do in the first part you also do in the second part, and as long as the strides are "clean" and not half strides. Splitting the stride (when the horse's forelegs step either side of the pole) indicates a half stride distance and shows you need to fix the canter (either increase or decrease it by half a stride length).

EXERCISE 3: PRACTICING ADJUSTABILITY

This exercise should not be attempted until you and your horse can set up and maintain the same stride length in both parts comfortably and without force. If the horse gets heavy, you will open the hip angle, use your back/core and apply direct rein aids. If the horse gets weak, shoulders back and leg, move up.

Exercise 3

- 4 to 3: Canter the poles in 4 strides in the first part and 3 strides in the second part.
- Ride a neat change of direction.
- 3 and 3: Canter the poles in 3 and 3 strides.
- Ride a neat change of direction.
- 4 and 4: Canter the poles in 4 and 4 strides.
- Ride a neat change of direction.
- 3 to 4: Canter the poles in 3 and 4 strides.
- Halt in a straight line.

KEY POINTS ▬ ▬ ▬ ▬ ▬ ▬ ▬ ▬ ▬

Do not assume the horse's canter will stay the same through the line — it most likely won't.

Exercise 3 requires feel, counting and conviction. Hoping won't make it happen.

Exercise 3: Strategy

Establish the canter for the first part of the line and, depending on the task, either maintain or change the canter stride length when you ride over the middle pole.

- **4 to 3:** When riding the 4 to 3 strides, you increase the stride length within the line. Close the leg, maintain the upper body in a two-point position, ride leg to hand and, over the middle pole, you increase or open the stride (lengthen). Remember, it is the leg aid that increases stride length. Leaning is not an aid.

- During the recovery phase ensure your horse doesn't continue opening the stride through the turn and prepare it for the change of direction either a simple change or a flying change of lead.

- **3 and 3:** To ride the line in 3 and 3 strides, you set up a more open canter (increase or lengthen) and maintain what you have through the line. Since the previous line required the horse to increase the stride length within the line, the horse might assume it should do it again. This time you have to maintain the stride using your position and direct rein aids. Use the recovery phase again to establish balance, rhythm and straightness and pace.

- Change direction with a simple change through the walk in a three-point position. It is best to ride a simple change (downward transition) before riding the line in the closed 4 strides.

- **4 and 4:** Ride the line in 4 and 4 strides. Set up a closed canter and maintain that in the line. It teaches your horse to wait. Ride this in a shallow two-point (a light seat) and use direct rein aids where necessary.

- Change direction with a simple change of lead. If the horse has become heavy or strong, ride a neat, straight halt and rein back.

- **3 to 4:** To ride the 3 to 4 strides, this requires a decrease or shortening of the stride length within the line, and this is the hardest ride.

- Finish neatly with a correct downward transition.

Jenny Randall and Nero Bello.
Photo credit: Trewey's Photography.

JENNY RANDALL New Zealand

Something I really appreciate is that Jen gives me exercises and things I can take away with me to practice at home. Jen demands excellence and makes me want to work hard. I have just started competing up to 1.30m — never dreamt I would jump that big but, thanks to Jen's encouragement, I realised I can do it!

*Independent training
promotes self reliance.*

Chapter 5
Improving Your Horse's Technique

Caroline Coop and Eye Wonder. Photo credit: www.kampic.com.

CAROLINE COOP New Zealand

Jen is very particular about basics being correct and having a structured, progressive training program. Stride control on a 60ft line is my bible.

 Correct position and structured training programs = success.

IMPROVING THE JUMP

Once the horse can jump individual jumps, gymnastics increase the horse's education. Gymnastic exercises are an essential part of the rider's and horse's education.

Gymnastic exercises are the most effective way to incorporate collection into jumping.

By definition, a gymnastic exercise is a series of poles and/or jumps in a row. The type and the height of the jumps, as well as the distances between the jumps, vary according to the skill being taught or refreshed.

New skills can be taught more easily because of continued repetition of the same exercise.

The bascule — in theory, the horse's body should form a perfect arc over the jump. The highest point of the horse's arc should be directly over the highest point of the jump.

The Ideal Bascule (Arc)

The horse's shape (how he uses his body) over the jump is the direct result of three things:

1. The type of jump (vertical, oxer, triple bar, etc.).
2. The ride to the jump (balance, rhythm, straightness and pace).
3. The rider's position.

The highest point of the horse's bascule (arc) should be over the highest point of the jump.

Vertical   Ascending Oxer   Square Oxer

In theory, the horse's body should form a perfect arc over the jump (which is termed 'bascule'). Unfortunately, not all horses know the theory nor do they conform to our ideal.

Fortunately, with planned and progressive training on the flat and over jumps, we can improve and develop the horse's jumping technique.

Gymnastic Exercises:

Gymnastic exercises are good for both, riders and horses. Once the horse understands the gymnastic exercise, it will find the correct distance (take-off point), as long as it is an appropriate exercise and it is measured correctly.

The related distances allow the rider to focus on position. In gymnastics, horse and rider can jump bigger jumps without fear of having to get the striding correct.

Gymnastic exercises promote:

- A forward, calm and straight canter.
- Confidence in both rider and horse.
- Correctness of the rider's position and horse's technique over the jump.
- The horse's agility, straightness and strength.

The gymnastic I use the most is what I call the "cookbook gymnastic." It is simple to build, doesn't require much equipment, and it is non-threatening to both rider and horse. Build gymnastics progressively.

For horses, place three trotting poles at a comfortable distance for the horse's stride (approximately 4.6ft apart). At a distance of 9ft from the last trot-pole, build a cross rail, then vertical 18ft from the first. The last jump is an oxer built between 19ft and 21ft from the vertical.

For ponies, remove trotting poles and canter into the gymnastic.

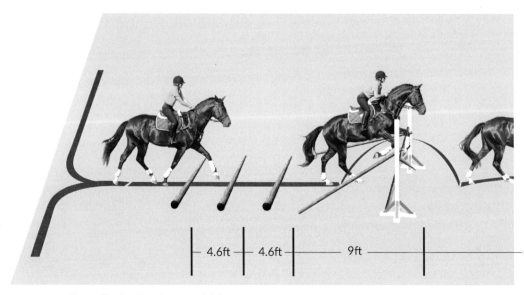

Above: The "cookbook gymnastic." Simple to build, and it is non-threatening to either the rider or the horse.

Purpose: For the Rider

The gymnastic should be set at a height so the rider and horse feel comfortable and non-threatened.

When both rider and horse are relaxed, the gymnastic example shown is an excellent exercise to work on:

- establishing rider confidence,
- correct rider position,
- eye control, and
- practicing the jumping releases (mane, crest and automatic).

Purpose: For the Horse

- Improves the horse's canter by establishing a rhythm.
- Helps to promote trust between horse and rider.
- Teaches the horse jumping technique.
- Teaches the horse that the jump takes over from the rider's hand (the horse learns to balance off the sight of the jump without the rider's intervention).

18ft — 19 to 21ft

Strategy

Trot forward and straight, maintaining a calm rhythm over the poles. Beginner or less confident riders should ride the poles in a two-point position. More experienced riders can ride the poles in a rising trot. Eyes should always be looking forward and straight — with conviction!

Once in the gymnastic, the horse will jump the cross rail, take one stride to the vertical, and one stride to the oxer.

Through the gymnastic, maintain position and the soft release — following the motion and allowing the horse to use its body over the jumps.

Photo credit: Horses and People Magazine.

KEY POINTS ▬ ▬ ▬ ▬ ▬ ▬ ▬ ▬

When setting gymnastics use a tape measure. Being off by a little bit can make a big difference. Practice new skills and refine old skills with gymnastics. Gymnastics can also help salvage horses or riders who have lost confidence.

The rider's leg gets the horse to the jump. The rider's hand — softening — allows the horse to jump.

Opening rein.   Guide poles.

It is a good idea to place guide poles on either end of the jump rail to encourage the horse to stay straight and to jump in the middle. If the horse insists on drifting off the line through the gymnastic, move one of the guide poles closer to the centre, and use an open rein to guide it back to the track.

If the horse is getting quick or doesn't begin to collect (shorten) its stride, place poles in the middle of the 18 ft and 21 ft distances. These poles will teach the horse to slow down and start to collect its stride.

As explained in the previous chapters, you must ride forward and straight away from the last jump. Ride your recovery time correctly and complete the exercise with a straight and correct downward transition.

JUMPING RELEASES

1. Mane Release

Used by beginners. The rider grabs the mane with both hands about a third of the way up the mane. This release helps the rider maintain position and stay with the motion of the horse while jumping. It helps hold the rider from falling back and grabbing the horse's mouth for balance. It is also a good release for experienced riders when riding green, unpredictable horses. God put a mane on a horse to be grabbed!

Mane Release. Karen Lyon and Lyon Lodge Kinder Surprise.

Crest Release. Jill Swain and Fiarmo. Photo credit: Tom Von Kapherr.

Automatic Release. Jen Marsden and Wee Geordie Photo credit: Budd.

2. Short Crest Release

The rider slides his hands up the horse's crest a few inches. The rider's hands (knuckles) are pressed into the crest of the horse's neck. This release provides support of the rider's upper body and allows an amount of control on landing from the jump.

3. Long Crest Release

A more exaggerated, longer release than the short crest release. The rider's hands slide further up the horse's crest — about half way. This allows the horse total freedom over the jump. It is a good release, combined with gymnastic training, to use on horses that are afraid to stretch and open their bodies at the jump. In the gymnastic, because the rider has given away contact with the horse's mouth, the horse learns to balance off the jumps — the jump takes over from the rider's hands and helps the horse to maintain balance. The downside of the long crest release is that it is over-used and often creates floppy riders.

4. Automatic Release

This is the most sophisticated release. The rider maintains a steady, soft and elastic contact with the horse's mouth over the jump. The rider's hands follow the horse's mouth and there is a straight line from the rider's elbow to the horse's mouth. This release affords more control and communication with the horse. This release requires perfect rider position and balance.

For gymnastics, the mane and crest releases are generally used.

Developing Collection (The Ability to Shorten)

Combined with an effective flatwork program, gymnastic exercises will help keep a horse at optimum athletic condition — making the horse supple, strong, elastic and soft.

As well as helping to improve your horse's skill, technique, strength and confidence, gymnastic exercises are the most effective way to incorporate collection into jumping.

Horses must learn to shorten and collect their strides and balance themselves on the approach to a jump and on landing. Gymnastic exercises — set at tight distances — teach the horse to collect it's stride and rock back on it's hocks before leaving the ground.

Through the repeated exercise of collecting and the rocking back on the hocks, lifting the shoulder and knees, and rounding the back, the horse develops not only the hindquarter, back and shoulder musculature required for jumping correctly, but also develops a habit of using these muscles correctly.

Correct muscling through a correct exercise program (on the flat and jumping) enables the horse to reach its full athletic potential.

In this case we only discussed a simple gymnastic. There are as many ways to build grids or gymnastic exercises as there are reasons to use them.

Important Considerations

It is extremely important to have a ground person when jumping — for safety reasons and to help you assess your position, and the horse's technique.

If your horse's jumping technique and/or confidence starts to disintegrate (i.e. your horse starts stopping or leaving a leg behind), this is an indication that the distances are too tight or the jumps are too high. The ground person should increase the distances between the jumps or lower the jump.

The purpose of gymnastics is to promote progressive and positive skill development for both horse and rider. If this isn't happening, re-think why you are doing a certain gymnastic. The problem could be:

- The rider interfering or not supporting the ride.
- The horse doesn't understand the skill being taught.
- The horse doesn't have the strength or ability.
- The actual type of gymnastic is inappropriate.
- The measurement is wrong.
- The horse is just plain tired.

 You must learn to recognize when enough is enough.
You can't learn everything in one session.

SAMPLE GYMNASTICS

All distances in feet (') and inches (")

Early Gymnastic

Approach in trot

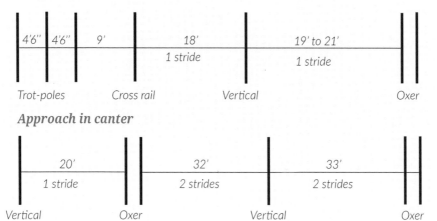

Approach in canter

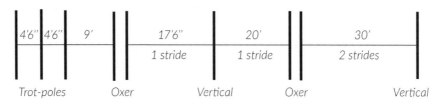

Intermediate Gymnastic

Approach in trot

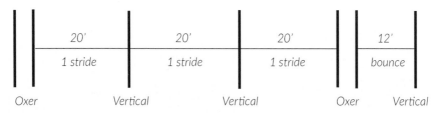

Approach in canter

Trish Pearce and Joan Jet. Photo credit: www.kampic.com.

Chapter 6
Problem Solving

Tim Pearce and Oracle WT. Photo credit: www.kampic.com.

TRISH AND TIM PEARCE New Zealand

Jen's coaching teaches a range of strategies that enables riders to continue to train independently using good core principles. Her basic coaching mantra of maintaining rhythm, balance and straightness removes a reliance on having a good eye. So, for many amateur riders, such as myself, who struggle to see a good spot if it hit them on the nose, it offers a way forward.

It's all about the quality of the canter.
GO FORWARD!

PROBLEM SOLVING

The following are two real life examples of some problems I have encountered. I'll explain how the rider, horse and I have dealt with these problems.

All horses are natural jumpers. Just ask any young rider who's jumped a horse bareback over fallen down trees, buckets supporting rake handles and just about anything else that can be found lying around.

Regardless of their natural talent, competition horses, just like human athletes, learn and improve through progressive skill development, and this requires laying good foundations.

First Things First

Before attempting to improve performance or resolve problems we need to consider the following:

- Is the horse sound?
- Are horse and rider capable of jumping the height and width presented?
- Does the horse understand the exercise or task, and is it appropriate?
- Is the rider helping or hindering the horse?
- Does the horse want to jump and/or is the horse jumping out of fear?

Since I know both horses and riders, I can assure that each horse is sound and athletically capable of jumping the jumps and that, given the right direction and training strategies, the rider is capable and confident enough to help improve the horse.

Flatwork is fundamental to all riding disciplines. For the hunters and jumpers it is a means to an end. Good work on the flat encourages the horse to relax and drop any defenses it might have developed. A well-balanced and supple horse that accepts the rider will consistently out-perform a stiff, resisting horse. Flatwork is a very important part of training for both horse and rider, and it should never be minimized.

Purpose: Flatwork for the Rider

- Teaches correct position (body control).
- Teaches co-ordination of aids.
- Teaches a feel for balance, rhythm, straightness, collection and extension.
- Teaches discipline and accuracy.

Purpose: Flatwork for the Horse

- Teaches horse to accept rider's aids.
- Teaches horse to become balanced, supple and elastic.
- Helps physical and mental relaxation.
- Conditions the muscular and cardiovascular system.

> *The hardest part about jumping a course is getting to the jumps and that is flatwork!*

David Colette and Buster. Photo credit: Angie Ivory.

KRISTA AND MISSY

Missy's Case Study

My first example is of a young Holsteiner-Thoroughbred cross mare named Missy, owned and ridden by Krista Foley. Here's what Krista has to say about Missy:

Missy was green and had an awful canter that was very strung out, covering way too much ground and traveling on her forehand. Using the reins to try to set her on her hind-end did not work very well, as she would either grab the bit and pull or she would want to buck.

In our early lessons with Jen, we spent a good deal of time using cavaletti to help her learn to compress her canter and rock back on her hind-end. I remember doing long lines of one-strides and bounces (including those set on a bending line). As well as those, Jen had me lunge her over a line of curved cavaletti at home to help teach her to balance herself and not leap across them.

When I first saw Missy, I thought that she could jump but, so what? The hardest part of jumping a course is getting to the jumps and that means cantering.

Missy really did have an awful canter. Krista looked like she was riding three horses – a head and neck out the front, hocks and a tail out the back with Krista sitting in the middle. The primary problem with Missy was that she was very weak behind and, therefore, uncoordinated and out of balance in the canter.

Missy was weak and couldn't carry her weight on her hindquarters. She dragged herself around on her forehand, and leaned on her rider trying to find support and balance. She had difficulty maintaining the canter for more than eight strides.

Training Strategy for Missy

The training strategy was to teach Missy to canter by improving her strength and coordination. Missy was cantered during hacks, on the lunge and over cavaletti set at bounce distances, as well as jumping over three and four stride distances in straight lines and bending lines.

Krista Foley and Missy. Photo credit: Mewbery.

Missy doesn't have classic technique over jumps. Her learned balance, strength and rideability are a direct result of hours of training and hard work. Combined with her natural spring and carefulness, Missy has improved her performance. Photo courtesy of Krista Foley.

STRENGTHENING EXERCISES
All Distances in feet (ft)

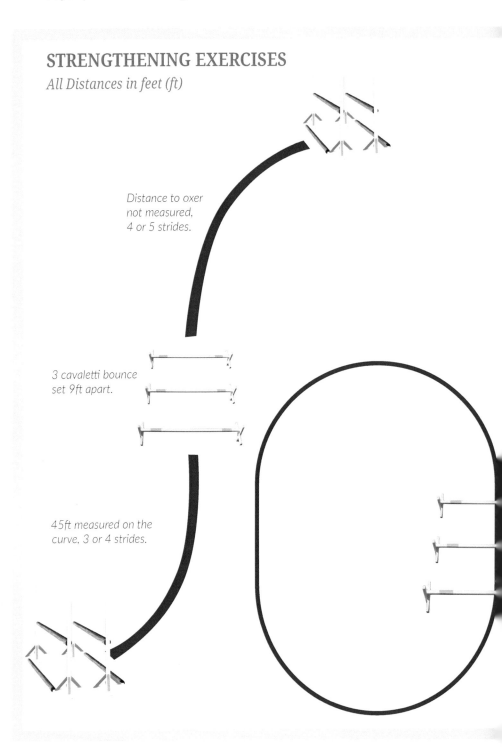

Distance to oxer
not measured,
4 or 5 strides.

3 cavaletti bounce
set 9ft apart.

45ft measured on the
curve, 3 or 4 strides.

During our early lessons, we spent a good deal of time using cavaletti to help Missy learn to compress her canter and rock back on her hind-end.

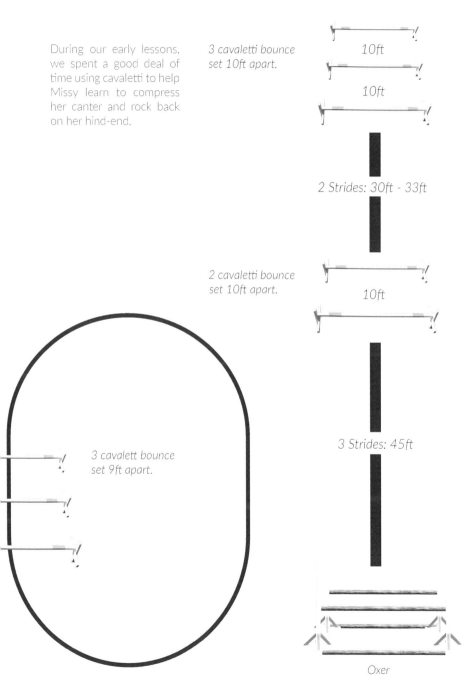

3 cavaletti bounce set 10ft apart.

10ft

10ft

2 Strides: 30ft - 33ft

2 cavaletti bounce set 10ft apart.

10ft

3 Strides: 45ft

3 cavalett bounce set 9ft apart.

Oxer

Serpentines and circles were added to the daily routine once straight lines improved. Stride control over poles and jumps were introduced, along with gymnastics for stride control, strength, balance and jumping technique. (Refer to Chapters 2, 3 and 4.)

Missy cantered a lot and did lots of downward transitions to lighten the forehand, strengthen the hind end, make her respectful and teach her the half-halt. Krista and Missy worked hard together and, about six months later, we started to see a measurable improvement.

A greatly improved canter, combined with a good flat work and jumping program, has resulted in Krista and Missy representing their province, Nova Scotia, at the Canadian Inter-Provincial Championships in Bromont, Quebec in 2014.

If you look at the photo of Missy jumping, she is a bit loose in the front end, but she is excellent in the way she follows through behind. She can now canter to the jumps on a rideable and controlled canter. Her learned balance, strength and rideability — a direct result of hours of training and hard work — combined with her natural spring and carefulness are improving her performance and winning prizes.

Although I love watching horses jump in the classic bascule, sometimes you just can't have it, but, remember, RIDEABILITY is a very important element in show jumping and that you can achieve through good training.

We were so focused on Missy's canter and her jumping technique and my hatred of teaching in the mud and rain, that we forgot to train in wet conditions. It turns out that Missy isn't a "mudder" and, since horse shows aren't canceled due to rain, our next project with Missy was mud jumping.

JILL AND FIAMO

Fiamo's Case Study

Fiamo is an 11 year-old 16.1hh Hanoverian gelding. His owner and rider, Jill Swain, rode with me as a junior and started training Fiamo with me three years ago. Here's what Jill has to say about Fiamo:

Fiamo was jumping at the fences and not using himself properly. In the lessons, Jen set up three white plank jumps with a very tight distance between them to help him make his arc in the proper place and centred over the jump. It seemed to work very well and made him much smarter at this.

I was finding the distances between the jumps were riding very tight. Jen also changed my landing position, as well as keeping my eye up over the jump. It really helped me fit the strides in much better.

Fiamo's is a very scopey jumper. He is athletic, supple and jumps very clean. While this is a positive, problems arose when he started jumping bigger and wider jumps, with more complex combinations and distances.

The arc (bascule) of Fiamo's jump wasn't centred over the highest element of the jump. Fiamo was over-shooting the arc and his canter stride was getting too long in the first two strides away from the jump, causing Jill to be pulled out of position and unable to control the stride.

A scopey horse ridden by a talented or natural rider often gets away with having technical faults in the same way a rider on a scopey and very honest horse can get away with faults in their riding position.

As the jumps got higher and wider, it became very evident that Fiamo was over-shooting the arc — what we call jumping at the jump and not around it.

This is not uncommon and usually happens when a horse isn't strong enough in the hindquarters and, therefore, doesn't have the strength to rock back on its hocks.

The Ideal Bascule (Arc)

In theory, the horse's body should form a perfect half circle over the jump — this is called "bascule."

The highest point of the horse's arc should be centred over the highest point of the jump.

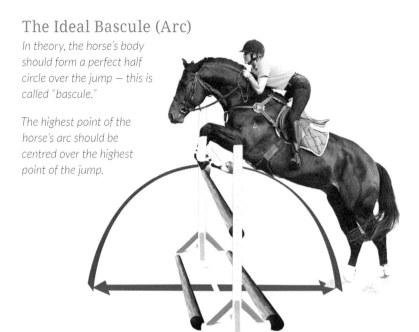

Over-Shooting the Arc

Over-shooting the arc causes the horse to land too far away from the jump, shortening the distance between jumps.

Over-shooting the arc also causes the first strides away from the jump to be long and flat.

Training Strategy for Fiamo

Fiamo's primary problem is the same one that Missy had — lack of strength and coordination and it has the same solution:

- Cavaletti exercises (see Missy's Case Study) for strength training combined with exercises to change the shape of the arc (bascule) and stride control.
- Exercises to change the bascule (the shape the horse's arc over the jump).
- Trotting to jumps.

Fiamo is a lovely horse made better through training. Changing his bascule so the highest point of the arc is over the highest point of the jump, has made Fiamo much easier to ride. Photo credit: Tom Von Kapherr.

Trotting to Jumps

Trotting to verticals set at a height of 1.10m and over teaches:

- The horse to go deep and curl (bascule) around the vertical by rocking back on it's hocks, developing strength and changing the technique.
- The rider to maintain balance, rhythm, straightness, position and be patient. Trotting to jumps really teaches the rider to use their eyes for balance, direction and conviction to jump the jump.

FURTHER EDUCATION
All Distances in feet (ft)

Line jumped in both directions.

The 22ft between the planks is tight and the 60ft distance allows 4 or 5 canter strides.

The exercise was varied as follows:

- Gymnastic to oxer in 4 strides
- Oxer to gymnastic in 5 strides
- Gymnastic to oxer in 5 strides
- Oxer to gymnastic in 4 strides.

The last one is the most difficult ride because of the distance between the planks, the height of jumps and width of the oxer.

Plank

22ft (1 stride)

Plank

22ft (1 stride)

Plank

60ft

Oxer

Gymnastics

Just as Krista and Missy, Jill and Fiamo practiced cavaletti exercises at home. During the coaching sessions we focused on stride control in and away from gymnastics.

We first introduced the three planks at 22ft apart. They were set at an easy height, with the middle vertical set 2 holes (approximately 3in) higher than the first and last. The 22ft distance means one stride. Fiamo found it very difficult to jump such a short distance, so we added placing poles half way between the jumps. This helped to slow Fiamo's momentum and taught him to rock back on his hocks.

Later, we added the oxer 60ft away from the gymnastic.

The vertical one-stride gymnastic is based on an 11ft stride. Going from the gymnastic to the oxer and riding the 60ft distance in four strides is based on a 12ft stride. This means that this line, ridden in four strides, requires an increase in stride length; from the 11ft in the gymnastic to 12ft to the oxer. This is the easy ride.

Riding the same four stride line in the opposite direction (oxer and 60ft to vertical gymnastic in four strides) requires a decrease in stride length. This is the difficult ride.

This line was jumped in both directions and the exercise varied as follows:

- Gymnastic to oxer in 4 strides.
- Oxer to gymnastic in 5 strides.
- Gymnastic to oxer in 5 strides.
- Oxer to gymnastic in 4 strides. This is the most difficult ride because of the height of the jumps, the width of the oxer and because the 22ft distance between the planks dictates a decrease in stride length from a 12ft stride to an 11ft stride.

For Fiamo, we also added placing poles half way between the verticals, to help slow his momentum and teach him to rock back on his hocks.

Strategy

The three vertical gymnastic at 22ft is a tight distance and it was a challenge for Fiamo, so we had him canter from the plank gymnastic to the oxer in the easy four strides.

Going in the opposite direction, Jill had to shorten the stride and ride the 60ft in five strides — setting up the correct canter stride on the short side of the arena to enable the extra stride to be added in the 60ft. This made the tight vertical gymnastic easier to ride and we were also teaching Fiamo to control his stride on the landing side of the oxer.

Once Fiamo understood the exercise — slowing down at the vertical gymnastic so he could curl around the jumps and going forward to the oxer and opening his body to jump the width — we educated him even more by changing the number of strides within the 60ft line, going in both directions.

The verticals jumped from a tight distance taught Fiamo to slow down at the base of the jump, rock back on his hindquarters, push and curl around the jump — improving the shape of the jump (bascule) and controlling the first strides on landing.

Riding the 60ft distance in four and five strides increased his rideability, and taught Fiamo to judge distances.

The change in Fiamo's jumping style — the highest point of the arc was over the highest point of the jump — made him much easier to ride.

Jill's position improved because she could follow the smooth arc of the jump, and Fiamo's stride was easier to control on landing and between jumps. Jill also had to remember to keep her chin up over the jumps and on landing, so she wouldn't collapse her position.

In Summary

Missy and Fiamo are lovely horses made better through training. Two different problems but both arising from the same root cause, they were not strong enough in the hindquarters. Both problems were basically solved with the same exercises adapted to their individual needs:

- Correcting rider position.
- Stride control.
- Gymnastics.
- Patience and correct training.

Correct training is about correct repetition — not drilling the horse to death. It requires designing and integrating specific training exercises into your flatwork and jumping program.

The key training principles are:

- **Training time:** High frequency — low intensity.
- **Competition time:** High intensity — low frequency.

What does this mean?

Training requires a high frequency of correctly practicing a skill to make it a learned skill (to make it a good habit).

If you only practice a new skill once a week, the skill won't become a learned skill.

High frequency means the skill is practiced daily or at least three times a week (i.e. little and often).

Competition, on the other hand, is a high intensity time and is not done daily. Once the competition period starts, the daily riding is meant to keep up fitness and maintain skills.

If the horse is over-trained at this time, the horse often becomes sore and sour. Get out of the arena and go for hacks. Let the horse enjoy itself so it will continue to enjoy its job.

Remember to train your horse to be calm, forward and straight.

KEY POINTS ▬ ▬ ▬ ▬ ▬ ▬ ▬ ▬ ▬

Correct training is about correct repetition — not drilling the horse to death. It requires designing and integrating specific training exercises into your general flat work and jumping program.

Rideability is an important element in show jumping. The biggest scope and talent is meaningless if you can't get to the jump!

Jill Swain and Fiamo. Photo credit: Jensen Shoebridge Photography.

Every time you ride you should ride to the best of your ability, practice correctness and establish good habits. Habits are the foundation of your riding and you want to build a good, strong and correct foundation.

Jill Swain and Fiamo. Photo credit: Tom Von Kapherr.

> *Horses become brave
> with educated and
> brave riders.*

MONICA OAKLEY and LAX. New Zealand. Photo credit: Take The Moment Photography.

Chapter 7
Developing Your
Options On-Course

Merran Hain and Tregonning. Photo credit: Courtesy of NZ Horse & Pony Magazine.

MERRAN HAIN New Zealand

I believe you need to have regular tuition, otherwise you become less effective and drift into a false feeling of security. Because I have had training from Jen for the past twenty years, she is quick to recognise faults developing, especially in my case not riding forward. Jen teaches realistic goals for your level of achievement.

  The horse is the best judge of a rider.

WHAT MAKES YOU A WINNER?

Whenever I run clinics with competition showjumpers or event riders, I always ask: "Are you any good as a rider?"

The usual response is a bit wishy washy. I personally think a great answer is: "Yes and I'm working to get better!"

Then I ask a second question: "What makes you and your horse winners?"

The usual answer I receive from riders is all about what they can't do; what they're not very good at. I find it interesting that riders know their weaknesses so well and they want to tell me all about them. I always respond that there is no point in telling me what their weaknesses are because they advertise them!

Most riders (apart from professional riders), really only think and worry about their weaknesses, not their strengths. How can you win if you don't know what your and your horse's combined strengths are?

You win because of your combined strengths — not because of your weaknesses!

Training is about setting up exercises to turn a weakness into a strength based on the principles of balance, rhythm, straightness and pace.

At a competition, the course designer sets the track and type of jumps to ask horse-rider combinations specific questions, such as how to ride a line, how to turn, etc.

- The strategy of the ride is based on the course walk.
- The course walk presents the options available.
- Training makes the options rideable.

Previous chapters in this book have dealt with rider position, rein aids, using the short side of the arena and riding the track. Hopefully, these skills have been practiced correctly and are starting to be internalized into good habits. These skills are the foundation of all aspects of riding.

DEVELOPING OPTIONS

All show jumping courses have options. This chapter will mainly focus on the jump-off, where the rider can take a risk to make time against the clock. In the jump-off, if there is an equality of faults, the rider with the fastest time is the winner.

The clock, however, doesn't just record which horse and rider combination galloped the fastest between the start flag and finish flag. The winner is the horse that takes the fewest number of strides between the start and finish flags — thus having a faster time.

Rideable Options for Taking Fewer Strides on Course

- Change the track.
- Slice the jump (jump on an angle).
- Shorten the turns in and away from jumps.
- Ride a bending line straight.
- Use the different stride lengths efficiently and effectively.
- Increase the speed.

Jen Marsden Hamilton. Photo credit: Cheleken Photography.

> *The course walk presents the options available.*
> *Training makes the options rideable.*

EXERCISE 1: SLICING THE JUMP (JUMPING ON AN ANGLE)

Slicing the jump is an appropriate option if and when the track away is taking the rider in the desired direction.

Exercise Strategy

When jumping a jump on a slice or angle, remember the track in gives the track away. Use your eyes to establish and hold the track. Use your eyes!

Preventing run outs: When slicing a jump, there is a wide angle side and a narrow angle side. The possibility of the horse running out on the wide angle side is there. To prevent this, use an open rein on the narrow angle side. On the wide angle side, the leg and a slight bearing rein will block any side motion or drifting, and keep the horse straight. Have enough leg to maintain the desired impulsion. Correct position and eyes with conviction will get you to the other side.

Practice riding the straight track away from the jump. Why take the risk of jumping the front side of the jump on an angle if you don't ride the desired track away?

Practice the exercise jumping the jump in both directions — left to right over the jump and right to left.

Any straightness problems on the flat will haunt you when jumping on an angle. Keep working on straightness in all your flatwork. Improving the way your horse responds to your rein aids and leg aids.

KEY POINTS:━━ ━ ━ ━ ━ ━ ━ ━

When jumping a jump on a slice or angle, remember the track in gives track away. Why take the risk of jumping the front side of the jump on an angle if you don't also ride the desired track away?

Any straightness problems on the flat will haunt you when jumping on an angle. Keep working on straightness in all your flatwork; improving the way your horse responds to your turning rein aids (open rein and bearing rein).

EXERCISE 1: SLICING THE JUMP

When jumping on an angle, there is a "wide angle" side and there is a "narrow angle" side.

The chance of the horse running out on the wide angle (in this case, running out to the left) is a possibility.

Hold the track with a soft bearing rein on the wide angle side and an open rein on the narrow angle side to hold the horse straight.

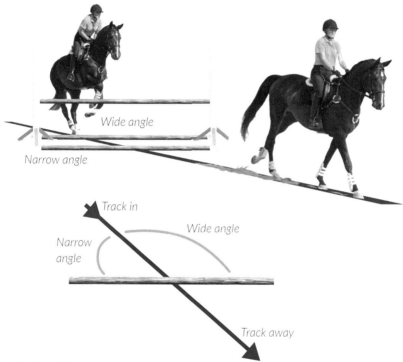

Wide angle

Narrow angle

Track in

Wide angle

Narrow angle

Track away

Rein aids

Bearing left rein: close the rein towards the neck and open the right rein.

When jumping a jump on a slice or angle, remember the track in gives track away.

Use your eyes to establish and hold the track.

The final conviction that you want to jump the jump comes from your eye. Use them.

Further Education

Practice the same exercise over verticals and oxers. Start low, and gradually make the jumps bigger and wider. You will probably find that the higher and wider the jump, the less of an angle you can take.

Be sensible and find out how much of a slice your horse will accept. How much of a slice can you take at the height you will be competing at?

Practice the same exercise off different stride lengths and at different paces (speed). Learn how much pace you can have on the slice. You need to know this if you want to be a winner!

This exercise is about teaching horse and rider to jump angles with confidence. If you ask too much, you'll scare your horse and teach your horse to run out or refuse.

TURNS IN AND AWAY FROM JUMPS

I'm often asked: "Did you see my quick turn into number 3?" I too often have to respond: "Too bad you didn't jump the jump."

Whenever jumps are sliced or jumped off short turns, there is always a risk. The aim of training is to lower the risk factor — a refusal, runout or knock down.

Less experienced riders like to take the risk of turning tight into a jump and then go wide away from the jump. This is too risky and it is not efficient.

You can make more time by turning quickly on the landing side of the jump — away from the jump — and it is less risky.

EXERCISE 2: TURNING AWAY

Place a single ground pole in the middle of the arena with six cones or markers on each side of the pole as shown in the illustration.

First, practice turning on the back side of the jump. Canter over the pole on a perpendicular track and turn after the third cone — Option 1, then progress to Options 2 and 3.

EXERCISE 2: TURNING AWAY

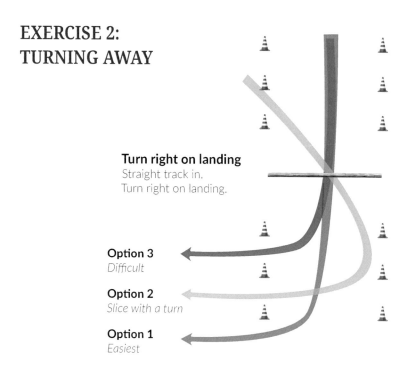

Turn right on landing
Straight track in.
Turn right on landing.

Option 3
Difficult

Option 2
Slice with a turn

Option 1
Easiest

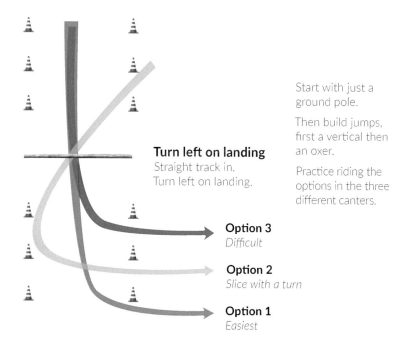

Turn left on landing
Straight track in.
Turn left on landing.

Start with just a
ground pole.

Then build jumps,
first a vertical then
an oxer.

Practice riding the
options in the three
different canters.

Option 3
Difficult

Option 2
Slice with a turn

Option 1
Easiest

Practice turning in both directions using the cones to help establish your tracks with accuracy. Practice options 1 , 2 and 3 in both directions.

After practicing over just a ground pole, build jumps — first a vertical then an oxer — and repeat the options.

Remember:

- your eyes establish the track,
- use an open inside rein to turn, with an outside bearing rein and outside leg. The open rein won't disturb the forward motion. The bearing rein and leg hold the outside of the horse.

EXERCISE 3: TURNING IN

Using the same ground pole placed in the middle of the arena with six cones or markers on each side, practice turning on the front side of the jump and cantering over the pole and away on a straight, perpendicular track.

- Practice option 1 in both directions.
- Practice option 2 in both directions.
- Practice option 3 in both directions.

Both the turns in and away must be practiced on different canters. How much pace can you have and still turn?

After practicing over just a ground pole, build jumps — first a vertical then an oxer — and repeat the options.

KEY POINTS ▬ ▬ ▬ ▬ ▬ ▬ ▬ ▬

Whenever jumps are sliced or jumped off short turns there is always a risk. The aim of training is to lower the risk factor.

There is no point in turning tight into a jump if you then go wide away from the jump — this is too risky (increases the chances of a run out) and it is not efficient.

Learning to turning quickly on the landing side of the jump — away from the jump — is more efficient and less risky.

EXERCISE 3: TURNING IN

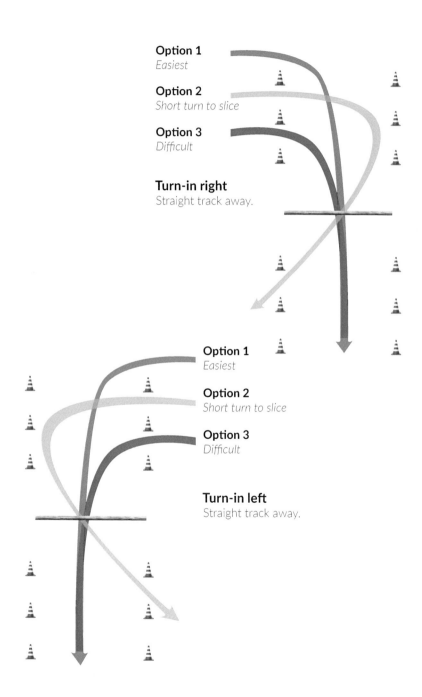

Option 1
Easiest

Option 2
Short turn to slice

Option 3
Difficult

Turn-in right
Straight track away.

Option 1
Easiest

Option 2
Short turn to slice

Option 3
Difficult

Turn-in left
Straight track away.

EXERCISE 4: PUT IT TOGETHER

- Practice the turn in and away, turning in the same direction — front and back.
- Practice turning in opposite directions — into the jump and away from the jump.
- Practice all the possible options turning in and away from the jump, i.e., come in on Option 2 and away on Option 1, etc.

Moving forward:

Both turns in and away must be practiced on the different canters (normal, open and closed). How much pace can you have and still turn accurately?

After practicing over just a ground pole, build jumps — first a vertical then an oxer.

Practice all the possible options and combinations, turning in both directions and on the different canters (normal, open and closed) and, more importantly, determine how much pace you can have and still turn with balance.

KEY POINTS ▬ ▬ ▬ ▬ ▬ ▬ ▬ ▬

Turning exercises are great fun, but if they are practiced too often and with too many repetitions, both the rider and the horse go crazy!

Practice 2 or 3 times and then do straight line work.

There are enough crazy jumping horses/ponies in the world already.

EXERCISE 4: PUTTING IT TOGETHER

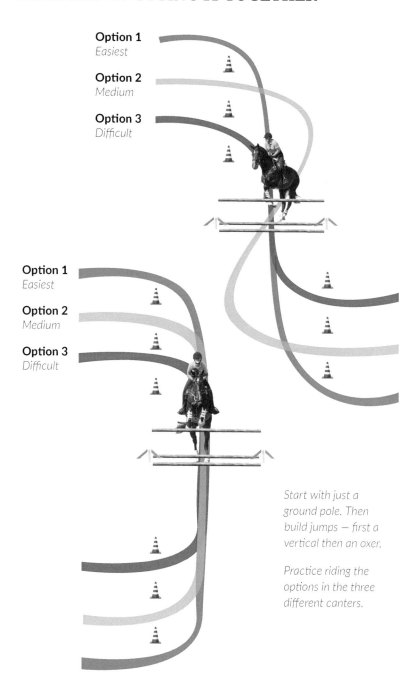

Option 1
Easiest

Option 2
Medium

Option 3
Difficult

Option 1
Easiest

Option 2
Medium

Option 3
Difficult

Start with just a ground pole. Then build jumps — first a vertical then an oxer.

Practice riding the options in the three different canters.

EXERCISE 5: ANGLES AND TURNS COMBINED

The exercise shown below is to help learn and practice turning arcs. Ride the exercise in both directions. How much space do you need to turn or roll-back on a jump? At what pace can you jump the jump while you and your horse remain balanced, calm, forward and straight?

- Option 1: Conservative (Green): A more reasonable option, using the arc of the circle to establish a good track to the jump.
- Option 2: Challenging (Blue): Very difficult, but with practice it is doable.
- Not an option! (Red): This is very difficult and carries too much risk (ie. refusal).
- Height and type of jump is a major factor in deciding the option.

EXERCISE 5: ANGLES AND TURNS COMBINED

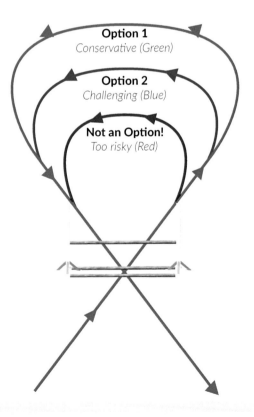

Option 1
Conservative (Green)

Option 2
Challenging (Blue)

Not an Option!
Too risky (Red)

EXERCISE 6: CHANGE THE TRACK TO CHANGE THE NUMBER OF STRIDES BETWEEN JUMPS

Set up a vertical and an oxer at right angles on a distance of five normal strides when ridden on a bending line as in Option A.

- Practice Option A, cantering vertical to the oxer in five strides on the bending line. Then practice this line in both directions: vertical to oxer and in reverse, oxer to vertical.

- Practice Option B — vertical to oxer. The vertical is jumped on an angle to establish a straight track to the oxer. Canter the line in five steady strides.

- Canter Option B in four strides. The vertical is still jumped on the angle, but off a more open stride. Practice in both directions — vertical to oxer and oxer to vertical.

EXERCISE 6: CHANGING THE TRACK TO CHANGE THE NUMBER OF STRIDES

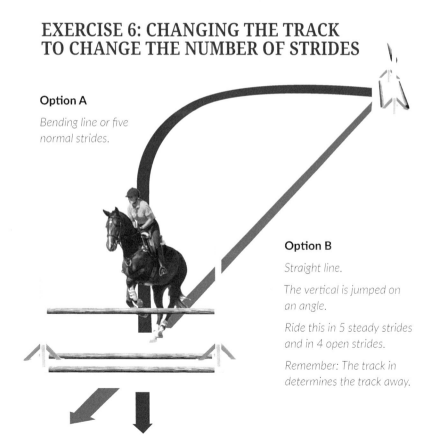

Option A

Bending line or five normal strides.

Option B

Straight line.

The vertical is jumped on an angle.

Ride this in 5 steady strides and in 4 open strides.

Remember: The track in determines the track away.

Two different, but definite, tracks are used in this exercise. Practice both options, making sure you have the definite track — either the bending line or the straight line.

Beware of the "never-never land" that exists between riding the bending line in five strides or riding the straight line in four strides — 4.5 strides is a non-distance. Be definite and accurate with your track and your canter stride. Short striding horses will be more comfortable on the middle track. Know your horse.

Efficient and Effective Use of Different Stride Lengths

A well-ridden, winning jump-off requires a confident, athletic, supple and rideable horse. The exercises in this chapter require different canters. The bigger the turn, the more pace you can have. Too much pace does not allow tighter turns.

Short canter — short turn   **Big canter — big turn**

A good and challenging jump-off has options. One option is to gallop the whole course and, if that is your only option, it can be dangerous. The galloping option is worth the risk to an individual jump if you can then control the stride after it or there are no consequences (if it is the last jump on course).

Points to consider:

- Progressive skill development — good training turns a weakness into a strength, which opens up the options available to horse and rider on the course.
- The course walk presents the options available. Training makes the options rideable.
- Speed is always the last element put into the jump-off equation — not the first!
- The benchmark is always calm, forward and straight.
- Course strategy is based on the horse/rider strengths. Pace, tracks to and away from jumps, strides between jumps, corners to be cut, and angles to be jumped are based on horse and rider skill level.
- You win because of your strengths — know your strengths and when to use them.
- Use your strengths to take fewer strides between the start and finish flags, and be a winner!

Angela Lloyd and Gandalf. New Zealand. Sir Mark Todd selected Gandalf as his 2008 Beijing Olympic mount. Photo credit: Barbara Thomson Photography, courtesy of NZ Horse & Pony Magazine.

Correct basic training opens the door to the Olympics.

Mary Petersen and Space Invader. Photo credit: Dot's Photography. January 2005.

MARY PETERSEN New Zealand

If you are fortunate enough to ride in a clinic with Jen Hamilton, remember it is a journey that equips you with skills that you can not only use in the arena, but take with you to use along the way through life.

 Horses trust riders who are consistent, ride with conviction and rarely present a gray area. 🙶

Chapter 8

The Course Walk

Nicoli Fife and Charlton Quiver. Photo credit: Courtesy of Nicoli Fife.

NICOLI FIFE New Zealand

I love the way Jen teaches horses to be more rideable with her exercises and riders to think more, which helps with show jumping and carries into the cross country. Jen is great. She makes me ride forward and be brave.

Nicoli was a member of New Zealand's first eventing team at the World Championships, Kentucky 1978. She competed at Burghley Horse Trials and other International events in the United Kingdom. She now breeds and produces horses for sport in all disciplines.

 Ride forward and trust yourself, the horse and the training.

COURSE DESIGN

At a competition, the course designer sets the show jumping course. This means he designs the track with options and sets challenges or tests for the rider and horse. The track and challenges should be appropriate to the level of the competitors and the class.

Course challenges/tests are determined by the types of jumps (verticals or oxers), the height and width of jumps, the measured distances between jumps and the track (the approach to and away from the jump or series of jumps).

Challenges have solutions. Challenges which have no solutions are traps — there is a big difference.

Course Designers' Test:

- The rider's education: Can the rider assess the challenge and communicate with the horse in an appropriate and timely manner?
- The horse's rideability: The horse's education or training.
- The horse's scope and talent.

All good show jumping courses test these three things. In my opinion, the course designer plays a major role in the education of rider and horse. Too many tough challenges, one after another, are demoralizing. Too easy a course doesn't promote learning and ongoing development.

Good course designers are our best friends. They respect horses and what they are capable of doing. They challenge us as trainers and riders. They are an integral part of our sport.

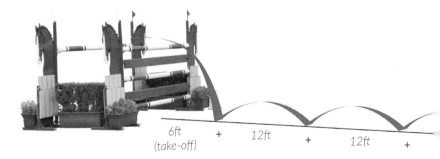

6ft
(take-off)   +   12ft   +   12ft   +

Walking the Course

Why?

The opportunity to walk the course prior to the start of a competition gives riders a chance to visualize where they are going (the track) and form a strategy as to how they are going to ride it.

How?

Before entering a competition, the rider must learn to walk distances or measure the distance between the jumps.

The average horse has a 12ft stride and distances between jumps are based on multiples of 12, this is why you should learn your 12 times table at school!

If the distance between two jumps is 72ft, then divide 72 by 12 and you get 6. Now you must take half a stride off for landing and half a stride off for take off. A half plus a half is a whole — 6 minus 1 equals 5. Therefore, a 72ft line is a 5 stride line as shown in the illustration below.

If the distance measures 74ft or 75ft, it means the line will ride in a forward 5 strides.

If the measurement between the jumps is 69ft or 70ft, it is going to ride as a steady 5 strides.

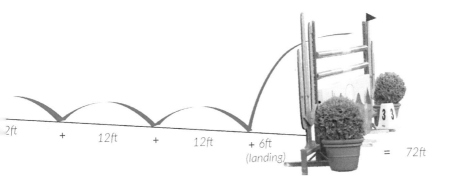

EXERCISE: STRIDING

Choose any area where you walk frequently and mark a distance of 3ft with tape.

- Teach yourself to stride a 3ft step between the lines — toe to toe.

Now measure a distance of 12ft.

- Teach yourself to stride 4x3ft steps between the lines.

- 4x3ft steps equals 12ft, which equals 1 horse stride.

- Practice your 4x3ft strides often. Make yourself as accurate as possible.

Mark a distance of 3ft in a place you walk frequently.

Stride a 3ft step between the lines — toe to toe.

When walking a line, since you want the distance to be measured toe to toe but the jump is in the way, start the first step with your foot parallel to the jump. After that first step, the next 3 steps will be toe to toe.

Fatigue and arena footing can affect the length of your stride. Never be afraid to re-check your step length before going to walk a course.

Measure and mark a distance of 12ft.

> *Teach yourself to stride 4x3ft steps between the lines.*

Photo credits: Archer Creative courtesy of Horses and People Magazine.

WALKING THE COURSE AT A COMPETITION

The course walk develops the plan and options; training makes the plan possible.

During the course walk, riders walk measured steps between the jumps to determine the distance between the jumps. Then, they have to translate this knowledge of distance into the number and quality of strides, which is related to the individual horse they are riding.

Unfortunately (or fortunately), not all horses have a 12ft stride all the time. This is a major factor when developing the course strategy. Know your horse!

"Two yanks and a cluck."

Cartoon by Ronnie Mutch. *Mutch about Horses*. Published by Lyons Press, 1978.

Straight Lines:

Take two steps to allow for the landing distance, now count 1, 2, 3, 4 steps (**one stride),** 1, 2, 3, 4 steps (**two strides)** etc, until you come to an even count close to the next jump.

Are there two more steps left to allow for a nice take-off?

- **Yes**: It's a comfortable distance — the type of jump (vertical, oxen, etc.) will determine the amount of impulsion/power required to jump it.

- **No**: Either lengthen the stride or shorten the stride as early as possible within the line (that's why we train!). Remember all the stride control exercises from Chapters 2 and 3!

Bending/Broken Lines:

These lines are still walked on the same step length. There are usually three tracks on a broken line:

1. The middle track makes a comfortable track that curves away from the first jump to the second.
2. The wide track to give more distance or making it safer into a combination of jumps — know your horse!
3. The short track (or a shaved/sliced angle) for shorter striding horses or when time is a factor.

Walk the middle track and then decide which of the three optional tracks is the best for you and your horse.

BENDING/BROKEN LINE OPTIONAL TRACKS:

1. The middle track

2. The wide track

3. The short track

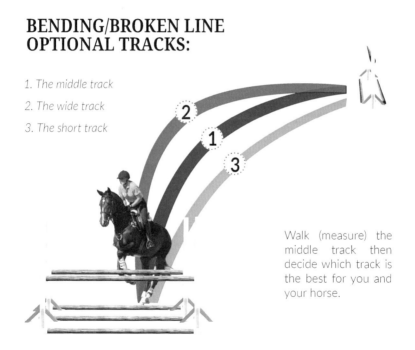

Walk (measure) the middle track then decide which track is the best for you and your horse.

Line of Two Related Distances

Course designer's test:

- The distance from the individual jump to the combination is 4½ strides.
- The combination is 2 strides at a comfortable distance.

4½ strides can't be ridden. It has to be ridden in either a forward 4 or a steady 5.

Rule of thumb solutions:

- Individual jump to combination: ride in the add. In this case the steady 5.
- Combination to individual jump: ride forward. In this case the forward 4.

Individual Jump to a Combination

Option 1: Steady 5 Strides

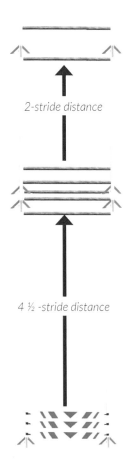

In order to protect the jumps in the combination, ride the line in the 5 steady strides. The jump coming into the line and its distance from the corner will determine the quality of the canter going into the line. Then, in the first part of the line, make sure you get "the add." You don't want to get there on the dreaded half stride or too long a stride.

2-stride distance

This option allows an increase of stride length in the combination.

Option 2: Forward 4 Strides

For big striding horses that have learned to collect their stride, riding the line in the forward 4 is certainly an option. Make sure you get the forward ride early in the line!

4 ½ -stride distance

This option requires a decrease in stride length in the combination.

Combination to an Individual Jump:

The type of individual jump after the combination and how well the horse jumped the combination must be considered.

Option1: Forward 4 Strides

For horses that jump confidently through combinations ride forward for the 4 strides. It is a natural ride.

Option 2: Steady 5 Strides

It is always better to add a stride early in a line than to ride frantically down a line.

The safest and most rideable option is based on the strengths and bravery of the horse and rider.

"Looks like a nice *flowing* six."

Cartoon by Ronnie Mutch. **Mutch about Horses**. Published by Lyons Press, 1978.

When you finally get there. There is no such thing as a bad distance. Support the distance with your position, eye and conviction!

COMPETITION DAY

The Course Walk

The class strategy should be based on the horse and rider strengths, not on their weaknesses, hopes or dreams. Factors to take into consideration are:

- Horse/rider strengths and weaknesses.
- Footing and slope in arena.
- Environment (distractions).
- Spooky jumps.
- Jumps to and away from the in-gate.
- First and last line — use the arena to generate the impulsion needed for the first jump.

You are Ready – You've Trained – Now Test the Training

- Memorize the course and jump-off — writing the jump-off on your hand is helpful. Check the time allowed.
- Before entering the arena, survey the course.
- Walk the course jump to jump in sequence.
- Check the start and finish lines, walk the lines and turns, and develop the class strategy.
- Walk the jump-off — determine where to make time, where you can shorten the track, etc.
- If possible, watch a few horses go.

Photo credit: Cheleken Photography.

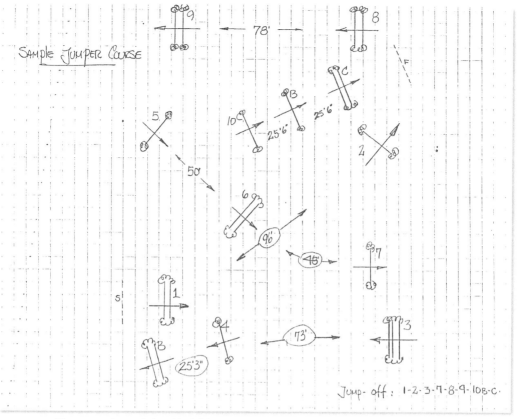

The course plan as designed by Michel Vaillancourt.

THE CLASS STRATEGY BY COURSE DESIGNER MICHEL VAILLANCOURT:

Course Strategy:

- **Fences 1 and 2** could be ridden in a direct 8 strides or bend in 9.
- **Fences 3 to 4A-B.** Number 3 should be ridden forward, as well as the first 3 strides in the line to allow the rider to balance the last 2 strides and protect 4A. At this point, 4A and 4B should ride normally.
- **Fences 5, 6, 7.** 5 to 6 will ride very forward in 3 strides, making 6 to 7 ride very tight in 3 strides. Staying slightly to the right would give more room in the second half of the line.
- **Fences 8 and 9.** This is an option line between a 5 or 6 strides, depending on the spread of the oxers. If the oxers are wide, the 6 strides would be an easier and safer choice, but the added stride must occur early in the line.
- **Fence 10 A, B, C.** This triple combination going late on course will ride a bit steady between A and B and pressing over C.

Jump Off Strategy:

Jump-off: 1 - 2 - 3 - 7 - 8 - 9 - 10B - C

- **1 to 2.** Conservative 8 or very forward in 7.
- **3 and 7.** Forward over 3 as tight as possible over 7.
- **8 to 9.** A bit wide over 8, forward 5 strides to 9.
- **10 B, C.** A very careful ride at 10B and normal at C.

So, do you agree with the course designer's strategies?

Final Thoughts on Course Walking

Training is about education. As you train with correctness, you and your horse gain skills, options, confidence, increased levels of communication and trust.

The previous chapters were about progressive skill development to promote the rider's feel, ability to read a situation, correct and timely communication with the horse, and a correct response from the horse.

The horse doesn't walk the course, the rider does. It is the rider's responsibility to develop an appropriate class strategy based on the rider/horse skill level at that moment. Riders who get greedy and ask a horse to do something it hasn't been trained to do are selfish.

The course walk presents the options available. Training makes the options rideable. Remember that just because an option is there, it doesn't mean it's an appropriate option.

Horses are very special and trusting animals — make sure you deserve their trust.

SHOW TIME!

My father taught me, when I was very young: Go out and have a good time, winners have the best time.

Devon van Til and Winterberg. Photo credit: Sophie Simson Photography.

DEVON VAN TIL New Zealand

Jen is a fabulous mentor and inspires me to be better in everything I do. I thoroughly enjoy her attitude and humor, making lessons challenging and fun.

Correct practice and equipment go hand in hand. The right bit with the right hands can improve the ride.

Jennifer Sarsfield and Ozaria. *Horse and rider team from the Chapter 1 demonstration.*
Photo credit: Victoria Clermont.

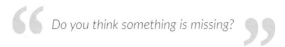

Do you think something is missing?

©CEALY TETLEY 2016

Jennifer Sarsfield and Iron Man. Photo credit: Victoria DeMore Photography LLC.

JENNIFER SARSFIELD Nova Scotia, Canada.

With Jen's coaching I have gone from Pony Clubber to a Grand Prix rider. She always recognizes cleanliness of tack and horse and an effort put forth by the rider to present themselves in tidy, appropriate attire. She has always been a supporter and mentor to me in my riding and also in my business at Medford Meadows Stable.

Honest assessment of competition performance helps fine tune skills and produce stars!

Suzie Hayward and Andretti. Photo credit: Cornege Photography.

SUZIE HAYWARD New Zealand

 ...we must never forget, every time we sit on a horse, what an extraordinary privilege it is: to be able to unite one's body with that of another sentient being, one that is stronger, faster and more agile by far than we are, and at the same time, brave, generous, and uncommonly forgiving.

— William Steinkraus, Olympic gold medalist.

Lady Olivia Waddy and Bosun. Competing at Tauherenikau International ODE. National advanced points winner for the year. Photo credit: Barbara Thomson Photography.

LADY OLIVIA WADDY New Zealand

Jen has taught me a sack-full of very sound jumping skills. As a coach myself, if I could emulate half of her coaching skills and knowledge I would be very happy.

 A passion for the sport will carry you far.

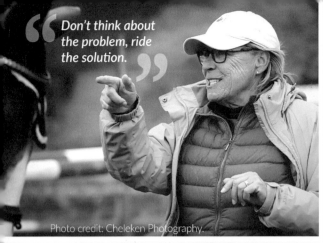

"Don't think about the problem, ride the solution."

Photo credit: Cheleken Photography.

"Is the horse ignoring you, or are you ignoring me?"

Photo credit: Cheleken Photography.

"Whatever you do; do it with conviction!"

Photo credit: Cheleken Photography.

"Today was a good day, no falls, no tears!"

Photo credit: Horses and People Magazine.

"Show jumping is about staying between the standards and over the coloured sticks."

Photo credit: Alex Petersen.

Photo credit: Alex Peterson.

I didn't get up this morning to watch you fall off, stop, cry or whine!

SO RIDE WITH CONVICTION! BE A STAR.

Photo credit: Mary Petersen

Riding should not be an aquatic sport!

Photo credit: Courtesy of Davina Waddy.

Riding is a non-verbal activity. Lessons are a one-way conversation, I talk, you listen.

Photo credit: Cheleken Photography.

CHELEKEN

Jen Marsden, 1958, 11 years old. First show riding Sister's Pride at the Old Chatham Hunt.
Photo credit: Carl Klein.

*Being able to just canter and let the jump
happen is the most important skill to learn.*

Chapter 9
Final Thoughts
From Basics to Big Jumps with Fun In-Between!

Jen Marsden riding Wee Geordie. Branchville, New Jersey. 1964. Puissance 6'6". Photo credit: Budd.

JEN MARSDEN HAMILTON Nova Scotia, Canada.

When running down to a wall you can't see over — you better trust the horse under you and the horse better trust the guy on top!

A Jump Ahead is based on a systematic progressive training program requiring discipline, focus, and conviction. I believe that basic skills form a foundation from which a rider can branch off to any discipline they want. Correct position and other basics enable safety, communication, and allows enjoyment while riding our favourite animal.

Winston Churchill, Ronald Regan, and others have been credited with saying, "There is something about the outside of a horse that is good for the inside of man." Who said it is unimportant. What is important is the sentiment.

When I was about 12 years old, my parents built our own three-stall barn and arena. Our property in upstate New York was surround on three sides by a privately owned bird sanctuary. It was heaven for me. I fed, watered, and mucked out stalls before going to school and then rode after school. My parents also helped with chores. To walk into the barn and be greeted by my best friends — and they were my best friends — was a wonderful start to the day. They knew all my fears and secrets and in their quiet way helped me through my teenage years.

Wee Geordie, the horse I jumped big jumps on while competing in the Open Jumper Division against professionals, helped me learn Latin verbs and noun declensions. I used to sit on him in the stall, backwards with my book on his rump and chant Latin out loud. Geordie probably learned more than me but I did pass the tests.

Jen Marsden Hamilton, recapping the day. Photo credit Alex Petersen

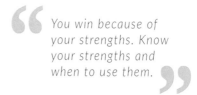

You win because of your strengths. Know your strengths and when to use them.

Jen Marsden Hamilton skijoring on Ratsky with Gail Morash Shea. Photo credit: Courtesy of Jen Marsden Hamilton.

Winter Fair, the chestnut mare George H. Morris described as a bad mover, was my junior show hunter and equitation horse. She might not have been a "daisy cutter" but she was a good jumper and lots of fun. When we weren't training, I fox hunted her, galloped quite dangerously through the bird sanctuary over homemade cross country jumps (my parents and GHM never knew about this), I rode her bareback in the snow and jumped snow jumps. Sometimes I even used Winter Fair for skijoring (a demonstration sport in the 1928 Winter Olympics).

Because of my very strong equitation position and rideable horses that trusted me, I lived through some dangerous and stupid stunts, but man did I ever have fun — and so did they! The horses and I had mutual trust.

I also did my own grooming and bandaging, even at shows. The first sign of spring was the horses shedding. I loved currying and brushing to reveal the beautiful healthy coats underneath and the horses enjoyed it even more. Bandaging was a time to check the legs for heat or swelling. The final mane pulling and clipping meant show season had arrived.

Before having our own stable, I took lessons at My Play Stables owned by Joe and Russell Stewart. They gave me a wonderful start and the opportunity to show Little Fiddle, the AHSA Champion Second Year Green Working Hunter of the United States.

I am a practicer. At our own place I practiced very hard, remembering what the Stewarts had taught me. When George Morris entered my life my practice became much more structured and focused. I redefined practice as training. George's teaching and my practice led to many successes in the show ring. I wasn't under George's eye daily or even weekly. I trained mainly on my own which is how I learned to take responsibility for my rides. I'd have a couple of days of lessons or a week and then go home and train, do self-critiques, and discuss it all with my father. Then I'd go back to George to be assessed and introduced to the next set of skills to be learned and mastered. Horse show competitions were the test of my training. Sometimes I passed and sometimes I failed.

I am a curious person by nature. What makes a winner?

In the 1960's there were no videos of great riders to study and dissect, no magazines with instructional articles, and very few readable books. If you wanted to learn it was up to you.

I became a watcher. Maybe even a stalker! I spent hours watching my heroes — Kathy Kusner, Rodney Jenkins and Bernie Traurig to name just a few. I'd watch them school, warm up and then followed them to the show ring. I tried to figure out what made them special other than their God-given natural talent. Each had a style and definite exercises and techniques. I tried to copy and incorporate my observations into my own program with mixed results. Over time I became much more discerning.

Becoming an accomplished rider or teacher/coach is an evolution. It takes curiosity, time, patience, correct hard work and guidance along the way. I've been fortunate. I've had more thrills of victory than agonies of defeat!

George focused and polished my riding and I continued my own horsemanship program. I practiced and trained hard but I also did my stable work and played with my horses. I was so lucky that I could. It was the combination of work, play, and trust that made me successful.

George H. Morris is a brilliant teacher and his brilliance recognized the cowboy in me.

Like all teachers/coaches I have developed a philosophy for teaching:

- Find the inner cowboy.
- Tame the cowboy.
- Never take the cowboy out of the rider.
- A tamed cowboy that can ride off the seat of the pants, when needed, is the winner!

Horses are wonderful creatures. Train correctly and at the same time enjoy recreation together. All work and no fun turns the horse and rider into dull robots. Always remember why we have a passion for our sport. It's all about the horse. Enjoy!

I believe that my ordinary horses did some extraordinary things for me because they were well-trained and looked after and especially because they loved me as much as I loved them.

Jen Marsden at 12 years old riding Little Fiddle owned by My Play Stables. Showing 1st Year green working hunter - 3'6". Fiddle was AHSA 2nd Year Green Hunter Champion in 1960. Those were the days!

Jen Marsden and Wee Geordie. 1964. Fairfield Conniticut. Photo credit: Budd.

Jen Marsden and Winter Fair. 1964 Madison Square Garden AHSA Medal Finals. Jen placed 4th in both the AHSH Medal Finals and the ASPCA Maclay Finals. Photo credit: Budd.

Jen Marsden and Wee Geordie. Madison Square Garden 1964, Puissance.
Photo credit: Budd.

As I tell all of my riders
as they enter the arena
— BE A STAR!